LONGMAN
INTERNATIONAL
TECHNICAL
TEXTS

TECHNICAL DRAWING 2
MECHANICAL DRAWING

A. Bankole
S. Bland

LONGMAN

Pearson Education Limited,
Edinburgh Gate, Harlow,
Essex CM20 2JE, England
and Associated Companies throughout the
world.

First published 1990
Fifth impression 2000

Set in 10/11pt Helvetica

Printed in China.
NPCC/05

ISBN 0 582 58857 X

Acknowledgements

We are grateful to The West African
Examinations Council for permission to
reproduce modified questions from
SC/GCE – Tech. Drawing 1 (Nov. 1977,
Nov. 1978, Nov. 1979, June 1980,
Nov. 1982, June 1983, Nov. 1983,
June 1984, June 1986, Nov. 1986,
June 1987) and *SC/GCE – Geom.* &
Mech. Drawing 1 (June 1973).

The Publishers are also grateful to the
following for their permission to reproduce
photographs:

Austin Rover Group Ltd. for page 32;
Barnaby's Picture Library for page 78;
Brenard Press Ltd. for page 66; J. Allan Cash
Photo Library for page 6 left; Format Partners
Photo Library for page 1 top; Hutchison
Library for page 1 bottom; Leslie Lane/Lane
Design Consulting for page 16 and Tropix/
V. J. Birley for page 90 top.

All other photographs were taken by Stuart
Bland.

Preface

This is the second of three books which
provide comprehensive coverage of
secondary school Technical Drawing
syllabuses. The other two books deal with
plane and solid geometry and building
drawing.

The books will also be useful as a
foundation to students taking courses in
Engineering and Architecture.

In this book we shall deal comprehensively with the principles of mechanical
drawing.

The book can be used either as a class
text or a self study work book.

Contents

CONTENTS

1. Drawing office practice

In industry and engineering, information is communicated by means of drawings and illustrations. For example it would be very difficult to describe in words the size, shape and workings of a motor car engine. The information required by engineers needs to be accurate and precise and technical or engineering drawings are used for this purpose. Because language is not used, technical drawings are understood throughout the world by people who speak different languages.

The drawing office is the heart of any engineering establishment; it is where creative ideas are formed and put down in the form of engineering drawings. These drawings are used by production engineers in the manufacture of components and by maintainance technicians who repair various mechanical components.

The production of engineering drawings does not require artistic skill (many drawings are nowadays produced on computers) but requires the ability to draw neatly and accurately with instruments, to visualise objects in three dimensions and to understand the principles of the various types of projection.

In order that engineering drawings can be understood by engineers throughout the world, certain international rules govern layout, type of line, dimensioning,

▲ Draughtswoman at work in a drawing office

▲ Computer drawing in an aircraft manufacturing company

printing, etc. The drawings in this book conform to the recommendations of the two main bodies that specify standards for engineering drawings. They are the International Standards Organisation (ISO 128) and the British Standards Institution (BS 308, Part 1).

The importance of standardisation

When a company manufactures a product, some of the components used will be obtained from other companies that specialise in particular components such as nuts and bolts, spark plugs, springs, gears, wheels and so on. This helps to reduce production costs because the manufacturing company will not need to set up special equipment for items that can be bought from other sources. It is obvious therefore that these 'bought in' components should be of a standard size, and reference tables are available for designers to refer to. In a large design drawing office there will be many draughtsmen, each concerned with a particular part of the complete design for a machine. The chief designer will be in charge of the drawing office and design work. However in a small company there may only be one designer and draughtsman responsible for all the work.

Presenting engineering drawings

Drawing sheets

Drawing sheets are based on the size A0 which is a rectangle of area 1 square metre. The table below shows the different sizes of metric drawing paper available and it should be noted that each succeeding smaller size in the table is obtained by halving the preceding larger one.

DESIGNATION	SIZE (millimetres)
A0	841 × 1189
A1	594 × 841
A2	420 × 594
A3	297 × 420
A4	210 × 297

Format

Drawing sheets have two formats:
1. **landscape** with the longer side in the horizontal position,

2. **portrait** with the longer side in the vertical position.

Line types and lettering

The various types of lines used in engineering drawing and their applications are shown below.

CONTINUOUS (THICK)	Visible outlines and edges.
SHORT DASHES (THIN)	Hidden outlines and edges.
CONTINUOUS (THIN)	Dimension and leader lines and hatching.
CONTINUOUS IRREGULAR (THIN)	Limits of partial views or sections when the line is not an axis.
CHAIN (THIN)	Centre lines, extreme positions of moveable parts.
CHAIN (ENDS AND CHANGES OF DIRECTION THICK)	Cutting planes, arrows indicate direction of view.
CHAIN (THICK)	Indication of surfaces which have to meet special requirements
DIMENSION (THIN)	Arrowheads should be sharp, black, and filled in.

ABCDEFGHJKLMNOPRSTUVWY
123456789
abcdefghijklmnopqrstuvwxyz

THE LETTERING ABOVE WAS DRAWN USING A STENCIL.
FREEHAND LETTERING SHOULD BE SIMILAR IN STYLE. IT CAN BE *SLOPING OR UPRIGHT* USING CAPITAL LETTERS. THE HEIGHT SHOULD BE 3mm, EXCEPT FOR

HEADINGS

WHICH SHOULD BE 5mm. LIGHT GUIDELINES MUST BE USED OTHER-WISE YOUR LETTERING WILL BE: UNEVEN AND UNTIDY

Border lines and title block

The drawing shows the usual position for your title block and border. The overall dimensions are given but these may differ if more information is to be inserted into the title block.

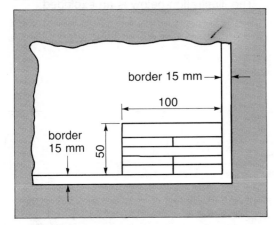

The enlarged drawing is a suggestion for the layout of the title block. Guidelines for main headings are 5 mm apart and subheadings are 3 mm apart.

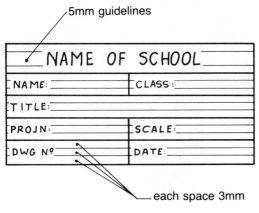

Again the layout may differ according to the information to be inserted in the title block.

Scales

To enable a drawing of an object to fit on to the paper, a scale may need to be used. For example very large objects would need to be reduced in size and very small objects would need to be enlarged. The drawing should be arranged so that it fits on to the paper, it is as large as possible and there is enough room for headings, notes and dimensions. Reference should be made to the section on scales in Chapter 1 of Technical Drawing Book 1: Plane and Solid Geometry.

Some common scales for engineering drawings

REDUCTION	1:2	Half full size
	1:5	One fifth full size
	1:10	One tenth full size
FULL SIZE	1:1	
ENLARGEMENT	2:1	Twice full size
	5:1	Five times full size
	10:1	Ten times full size

Symbols and abbreviations

The list of common symbols and abbreviations is based on BS 308, Part 1, 1984.

TERM	ABBREVIATION OR SYMBOL
Across flats	A/F
Across corners	A/C
Assembly	ASSY
British Standard	BS
Centres	CRS
Centre line	℄ or CL
Chamfer, chamfered	CHAM
Cheese head	CH HD
Counterbore	C'BORE
Countersunk	CSK
Countersunk head	CSK HD
Diameter	Ø
Drawing	DRG
Equispaced	EQUI SP
External	EXT
Figure	FIG
Hexagon	HEX
Hexagon head	HEX HD
Internal	INT
Left hand	LH
Right hand	RH
Machine	MC
Material	MATL
Maximum	MAX
Minimum	MIN
Not to scale	NTS
Number	NO.
Pitch circle diameter	PCD
Pitch circle radius	PCR
Radius	R
Reference	REF
Required	REQD
Round head	RD HD
Screw (or screwed)	SCR
Specification	SPEC
Spherical	SPHERE
Spot face	S'FACE
Square	□
Standard	STD
Thread	THD
Thick	THK
Undercut	U'CUT

Types of projections

Various different types of projection are available for use in engineering drawings. The most common is orthographic projection, either 1st or 3rd angle, and the number of different views will depend on the amount of detail to be shown. Pictorial drawing in isometric, oblique, axonometric or perspective projection is often used when an overall picture of the object is required.

Whatever method is used will require careful planning beforehand to ensure that the drawing is clear, can be easily understood and will fit on to the paper. The choice of projection will depend on the object itself and sometimes both orthographic views and a pictorial drawing of the same object will be produced. Hidden detail should be kept to a minimum and sectional views often help to reveal hidden detail. The different types of presentation will be dealt with in detail throughout the book.

Types of drawings

Detail drawing

This shows a single component and includes all the necessary information to define that component completely.

Assembly drawing

This shows two or more components in their assembled form. A number of subassemblies may also be fitted together to form an assembly drawing. A list of parts is normally included.

Combined drawing

This shows an assembly together with a list of parts, and details of the various components drawn separately but on the same drawing sheet.

General arrangement drawing

This shows the arrangement of the complete finished product which consists of a number of subassemblies and provides necessary information for effective installation.

Diagram

A diagram is a drawing which shows the function of a system, or the relationship between component parts, using simplified representation.

The illustration below is an exploded drawing showing how the various parts of the gearbox of a motor car fit together.

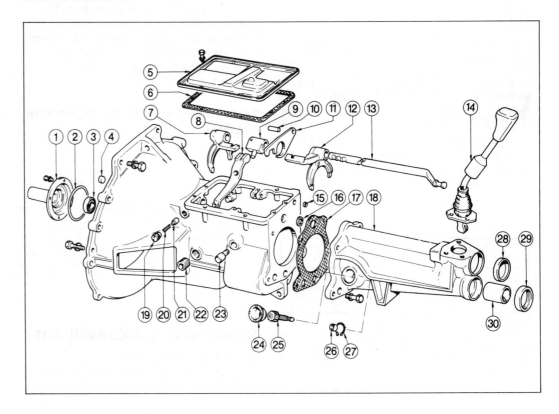

2. Pictorial drawings

Pictorial drawings are used to give an overall impression of an object; they are similar to a photograph. However because the sides are drawn at an angle, the shape becomes distorted. There are various different types of pictorial drawing and some have been dealt with in detail in Book 1.

Isometric projection

The sides are sloping at 30° and vertical lines remain vertical. Isometric projection is covered in Chapters 9 and 11 of Book 1.

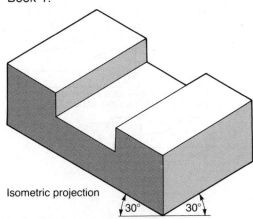

Isometric projection

Exploded drawings

Exploded pictorial drawings are often used to show how the various different parts of an object fit together. The illustration on page 4 opposite is an example of an exploded drawing.

Oblique projection

One surface is drawn to its true shape and the side and top are angled at either 30° or 45°. For cabinet oblique projection the length of the side is reduced by one half to make the drawing more realistic. Refer to Chapter 12 of Book 1.

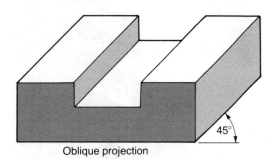

Oblique projection

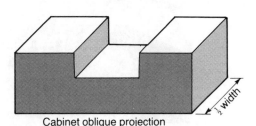

Cabinet oblique projection

Planometric projection

Planometric projection is often used by architects and room planners to show the inside of buildings. The plan is drawn out as shown to its true shape; it can be angled at 45°, 45° or 30°, 60°.

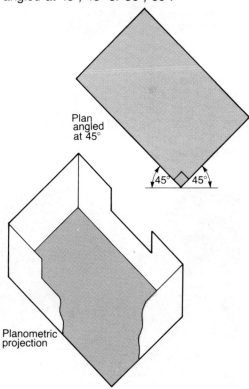

Plan angled at 45°

Planometric projection

5

Perspective drawing

Perspective drawings are drawings that show objects as they are seen by the human eye. How does this perspective drawing of a block differ from the pictorial drawings on page 5?

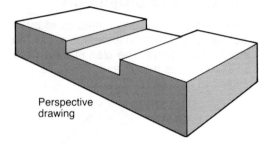

Perspective drawing

Vanishing point

You will notice on this photograph that the railway lines appear to recede to a point in the distance. This point is called the **vanishing point** and it is positioned on the **horizon**.

Distances

The distances between the balconies on this building become less as the vanishing point is approached.

Single point perspective

Only one vanishing point is used and the position of the observer will determine the position of the vanishing point.

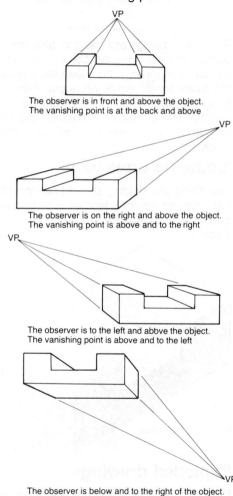

The observer is in front and above the object. The vanishing point is at the back and above

The observer is on the right and above the object. The vanishing point is above and to the right

The observer is to the left and above the object. The vanishing point is above and to the left

The observer is below and to the right of the object. The vanishing point is below and to the right. The underneath can be seen

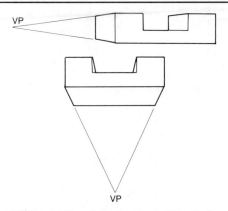

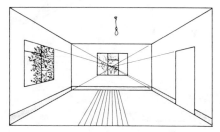

With the vanishing point on the extreme left or directly underneath, very little detail is shown

A single central vanishing point is used for this drawing of the inside of a room

Drawing in one point parallel perspective

When looking at an object the perspective outline can be visualised by looking at the object through an imaginary glass screen placed in a vertical position between the object and the observer. The perspective image appears on the screen where **visual rays** converge from the object towards the eye of the observer. The glass screen is called the **picture plane (PP)**. The position of the observer is called the **station point (SP)** and the eye

of the observer is called the **point of sight**. The horizon is an imaginary line in the distance which represents the eye level of the observer and the **vanishing point (VP)** is positioned on the horizon. The **ground line (GL)** is the intersection of the picture plane with the ground plane.

As the observer approaches the object it will appear to get larger. The picture plane is normally positioned between the observer and the object. Where the perspective drawing is to be larger than the actual size of the object, the object is located between the picture plane and the observer (lower illustration).

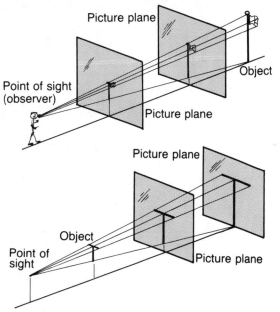

Location of the station point

For most objects the position of the station point should be arranged so that the sides

and the top of the object can be seen. For large objects the horizon is usually placed 1.6 m above the ground. To avoid too much distortion with perspective drawings, the station point should be located at such a distance that the cone of the visual rays will enclose the object at an angle no greater than 30°.

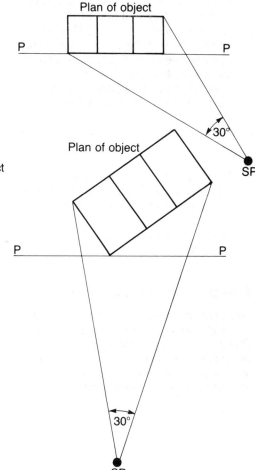

Procedure for drawing in one point perspective

1. Draw the ground line (GL), the picture plane (PP) and the horizon with the front elevation ABCDEFGH on the GL and the plan on PP. The plan is angled according to the position that it is viewed. The horizon is at a convenient distance from GL and its best position will be found by trial and error.
2. Locate the station point (SP) relative to the plan so that the cone of the visual rays encloses the object at an angle not greater than 30°.
3. From SP draw a perpendicular to the horizon to locate the vanishing point (VP).
4. From SP draw visual ray lines to the top points 1, 2, 3, 4 of the plan.
5. Join VP to points A, B, C, D, E, F, G. Project vertical lines from points 5, 6, 7, 8 on line PP. These projection lines will locate points at the back of the object.
6. Join up all the points to complete the drawing.

Two point or angular perspective

Two point perspective drawings use two vanishing points placed on the horizon. This is the most common type of perspective drawing and if you look at buildings you will notice that both sides recede to points in the distance.

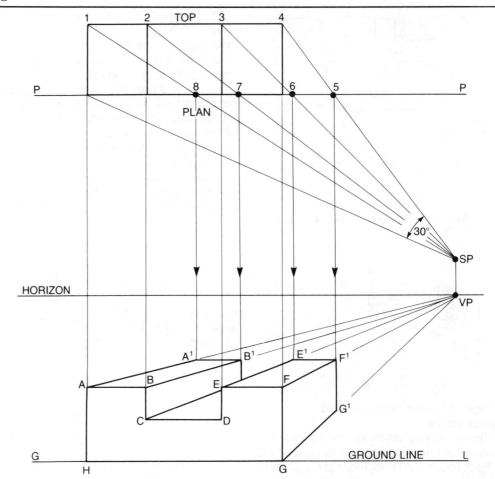

Procedure for drawing in two point perspective

1. Draw the ground line (GL), the picture plane (PP) and the horizon.
2. Draw the front elevation of the object on GL and the plan on PP (tilted at any convenient angle to PP). Project lines to AH as shown.
3. Locate SP relative to the plan so that the cone of visual rays encloses the object at an angle not greater than 30°.
4. To locate the vanishing points LVP and RVP, draw lines SP to P^1 and SP to P^2 parallel to the edges of the plan and project vertically to the horizon.
5. From points where the visual ray lines intersect PP, project vertical lines into the perspective view to give distances along the sides.
6. Heights are projected from the elevation to the nearest edge on the perspective drawing.
7. With all edges on the perspective drawing projected to the vanishing points the drawing can now be completed.

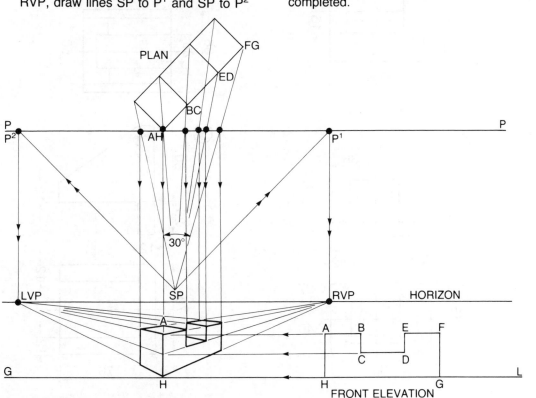

Exercises

For each drawing the plan and elevation are given in 1st angle projection. Using instruments and the measurements given produce:
a) a single point perspective drawing,
b) a two point perspective drawing.

As an additional revision exercise, you could draw each object in isometric and oblique projection.

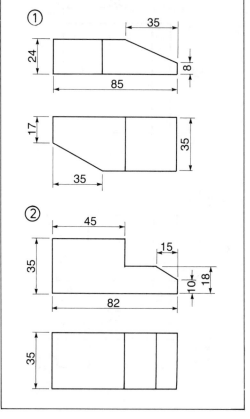

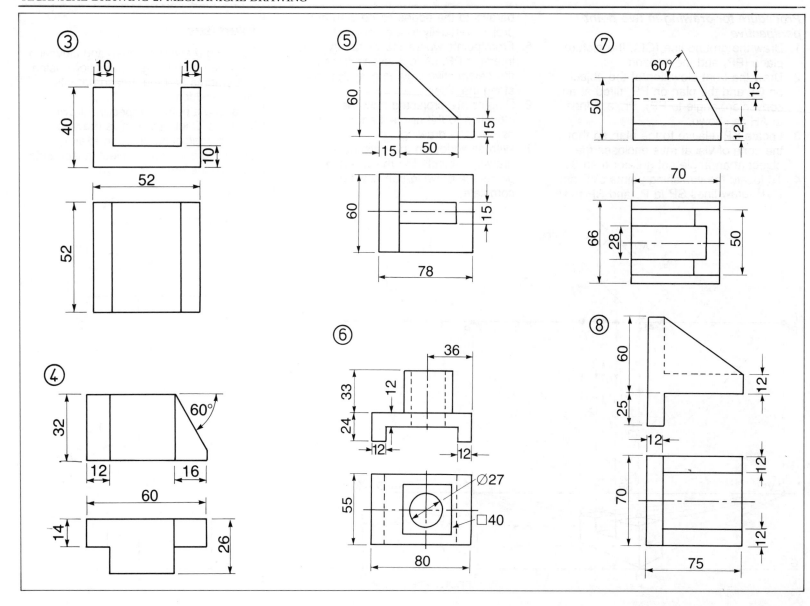

Three point perspective

A third vanishing point at the top is often used by architects and artists. This drawing of a building uses the third vanishing point to give an impression of height; the drawing also becomes rather distorted in shape.

The use of the third vanishing point will not be dealt with in detail because it is not a requirement of most examination syllabuses.

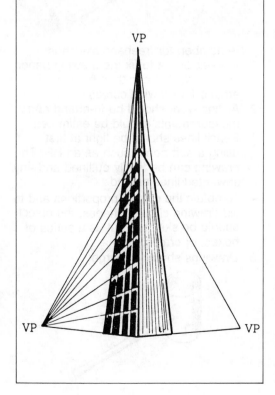

Estimated perspective

Often, when accuracy is not too important, a freehand or with-instruments perspective drawing can be produced. Considerable time can also be saved. The following rules apply to estimated drawings.
1. The vanishing points should be as far apart as possible and normally they should be positioned above the object.

2. Distances for height on the perspective drawing are marked off along the nearest edge.
3. The lengths of the sides will be foreshortened. The nearer the vanishing point the shorter the sides will be.
4. 'Midpoints' can be found by drawing diagonals as shown below.

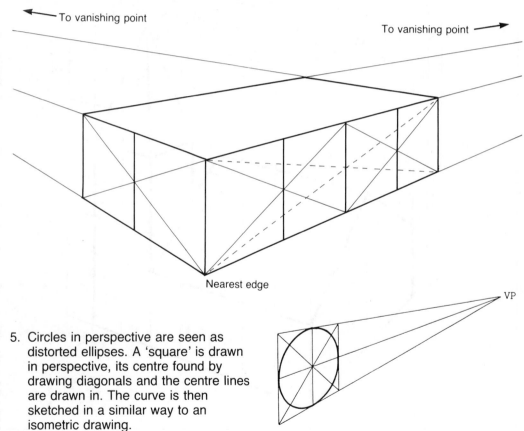

5. Circles in perspective are seen as distorted ellipses. A 'square' is drawn in perspective, its centre found by drawing diagonals and the centre lines are drawn in. The curve is then sketched in a similar way to an isometric drawing.

Using a perspective grid

To aid sketching in perspective, a grid is often used. An example of a grid is shown here and you can make a tracing of it to help you with your own drawings.

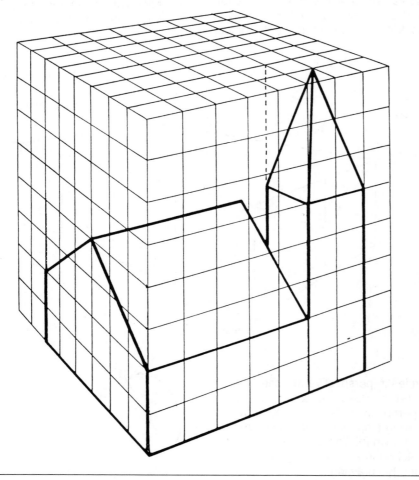

Freehand sketching

Freehand sketching was covered in detail in Book 1, Chapter 13. You may remember sketching the hide mallet shown in the photograph.

Remember, for freehand sketches:
1. It is easier not to fix the drawing paper to the board. It can then be moved around for drawing curves.
2. All line work should be freehand and measurements should be estimated.
3. Pencil lines should be light at first using a soft pencil such as an HB. The drawing can be finally outlined and any unwanted lines erased.
4. To obtain the correct proportions and to aid drawing circular shapes, the object should be sketched out as a series of boxes, or crates, first.
5. Drawings should be large.

Worked example 1: flat file

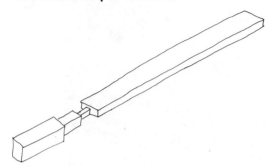

Stage 1 Sketch crates.

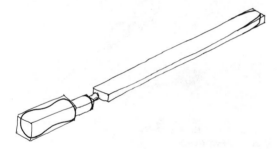

Stage 2 Sketch content of crates.

Stage 3 Thicken outlines and erase construction lines.

Worked example 2: hexagon head bolt

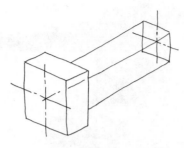

Stage 1 Sketch crates and centre lines.

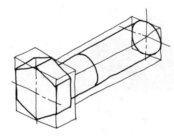

Stage 2 Sketch content of crates.

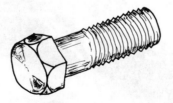

Stage 3 Outline drawing and erase unwanted construction lines.

Exercises: freehand sketching

From this list, and from any suitable objects that you are able to obtain, make freehand pictorial sketches. Your sketches should be as large as possible, in good proportion and use a variety of pictorial methods of presentation e.g. isometric, oblique and perspective.

1. Engineering tools
Pliers (various types)
Screwdrivers
Vee block and clamp
Dial gauge
Micrometer
Machine vice
Calipers
Drills
Surface gauge
Ball pein hammer
Different files
Tin snips
Hacksaws

2. Engineering components
Various nuts, bolts and screws
Taps and valves
Tool post on lathe
Lathe chuck and drill chuck
Tail stock of lathe
Motor car components such as bearings, drives, generator, carburettor, etc. which can be obtained from a scrapyard.

3. Engineering drawings
The plan and elevations of various engineering components are given in Chapters 3, 4 and 7. To help you visualise these objects, make freehand pictorial sketches of them.

13

4. Woodwork tools

These photographs show some woodwork tools which you could obtain for making freehand sketches. Remember to position the drawing to show as much detail as possible.

▲ Box spanner

▲ Spanner

▲ Hammer

▲ Sander

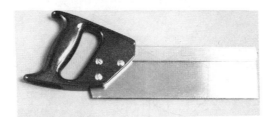

▲ Saw

▲ Plane

▲ Jig saw

▲ Screwdrivers

▲ Hand drill gears

5. General engineering components

You may be able to obtain from your school workshop or from a local garage various engineering items for sketching. Here are some examples to give you ideas.

▲ Pillar drill (cover removed)

▲ Hand press

▲ Plumbing fittings

▲ Nuts and bolts

6. Electrical components

You could sketch various electrical components.

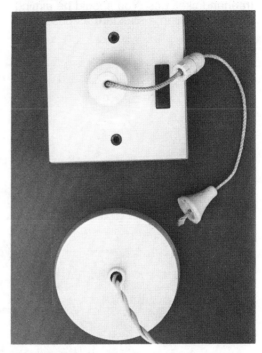

7. Around the home

There are many items around the home that you could use for sketching.

8. Professional design work

This photograph shows an example of design work for wrist watches using freehand sketches. You should be aiming to reach as high a standard as possible in your work.

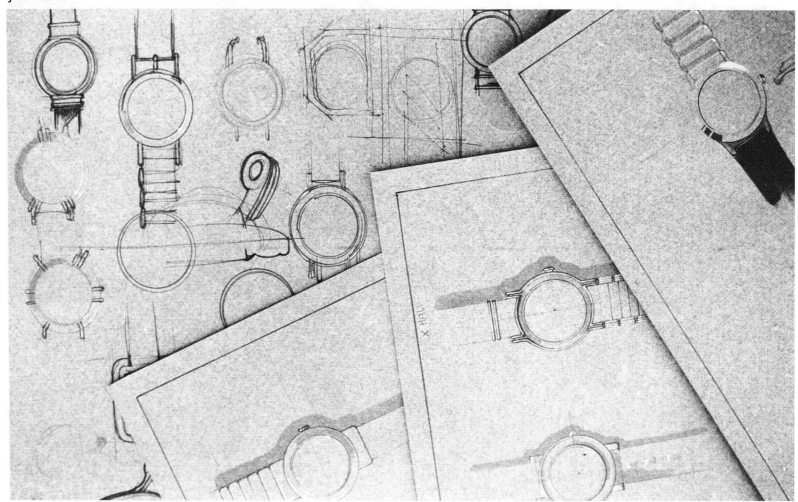

3. Orthographic projection

A full explanation of the principles of orthographic projection is given in Chapter 10 of Book 1. Here are some important points that you should remember.

First angle projection

The front and side are projected on to the vertical planes (VP and SVP) and the plan is projected on to the horizontal plane (HP). When opened out flat, the XY line represents the ground line or the joint between the planes. Drawn below is the graphical symbol for first angle projection.

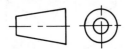

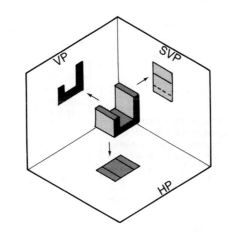

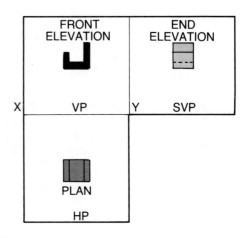

Third angle projection

The planes are represented by sheets of glass and the views are projected towards the observer on to the planes. The front and side are projected forwards to the vertical planes (VP and SVP) and the plan is projected upwards to the horizontal plane (HP). The XY line represents the ground line or the joint between the planes when they are laid flat. The graphical symbol for 3rd angle projection is shown below.

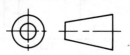

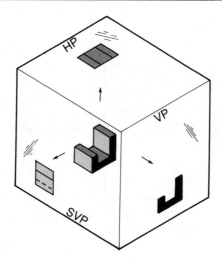

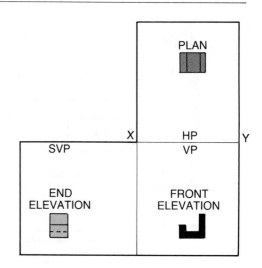

Presentation of drawings

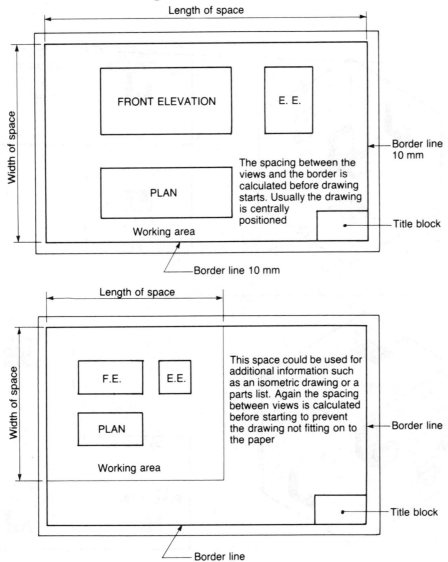

Length of space

Width of space

FRONT ELEVATION

E. E.

Border line 10 mm

PLAN

The spacing between the views and the border is calculated before drawing starts. Usually the drawing is centrally positioned

Title block

Working area

Border line 10 mm

Length of space

Width of space

F.E.

E.E.

This space could be used for additional information such as an isometric drawing or a parts list. Again the spacing between views is calculated before starting to prevent the drawing not fitting on to the paper

PLAN

Border line

Working area

Title block

Border line

Worked example 1

The isometric drawing shows a machined block. Using the measurements given, draw in 1st angle orthographic projection a front elevation, an end elevation and a plan. Your views should be correctly positioned and spaced well on the drawing sheet. Outlines should be sharp and dark, and construction lines should only just be visible.

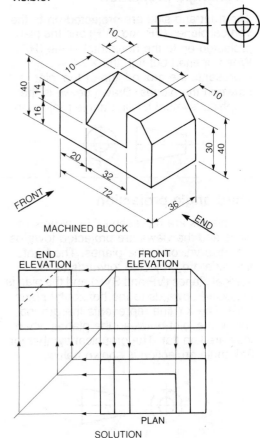

MACHINED BLOCK

END ELEVATION

FRONT ELEVATION

PLAN

SOLUTION

Worked example 2

The isometric drawing shows a bracket, and the orthographic views of the bracket are shown below in 1st angle projection.

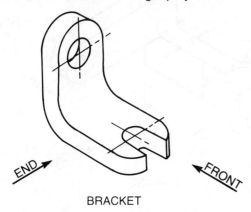

BRACKET

Revision exercises

For the six questions, draw the following views in orthographic projection:
a) a plan,
b) a front elevation,
c) an end elevation as indicated by the arrows.

Use a scale of full size or, if you wish, a scale of twice full size. Questions 1–3 should be drawn in 1st angle projection and questions 4–6 should be drawn in 3rd angle projection.

Add six important dimensions to your drawings.

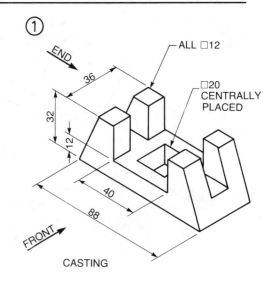

① CASTING

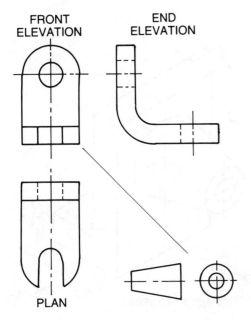

FRONT ELEVATION   END ELEVATION

PLAN

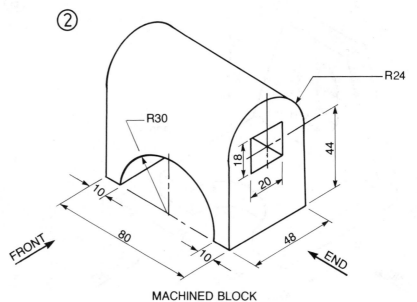

② MACHINED BLOCK

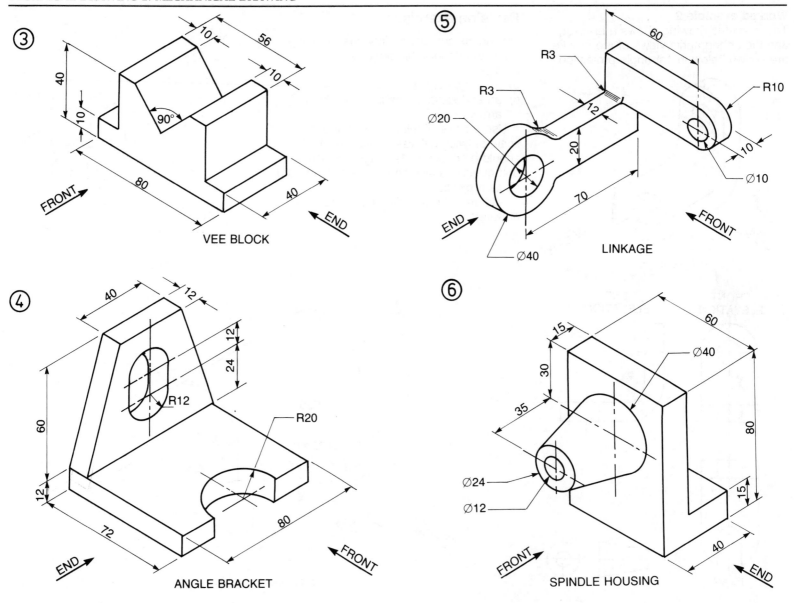

③ VEE BLOCK

⑤ LINKAGE

④ ANGLE BRACKET

⑥ SPINDLE HOUSING

Dimensioning techniques

Dimensions, or measurements, are essential on engineering drawings to enable the drawings to be easily understood. On engineering drawings millimetres are normally used and various abbreviations (see page 3) are used in conjunction with the dimensions.

Dimensioning rules

1. Extension and dimension lines are thin and continuous.
2. Small gaps are left between the extension lines and the features to be dimensioned.
3. Dimension lines have arrowheads at both ends. The arrowheads are sharp, dark and filled in. They are approximately 3 mm long.
4. Extension lines project slightly beyond the dimension lines.
5. Where possible dimension lines should be located outside the drawing, well spaced from the drawing and clear.
6. For symmetrical objects, or where sizes are repeated, only one half may be dimensioned.
7. Fillet radii and other small radii of less than 3 mm are sometimes not dimensioned. A note to this effect is stated on the drawing.
8. Dimensions should be written *above* the horizontal dimension lines and *above* vertical dimension lines when viewed from the right-hand side.
9. The symbols R for radius and ∅ for diameter are positioned *before* the measurement.

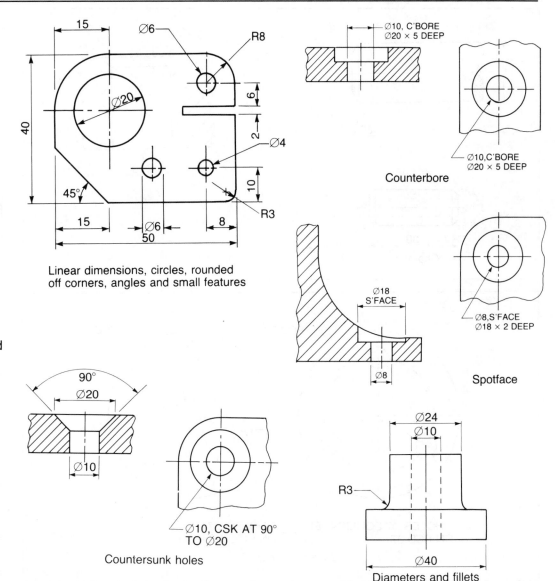

Linear dimensions, circles, rounded off corners, angles and small features

Counterbore

Spotface

Countersunk holes

Diameters and fillets

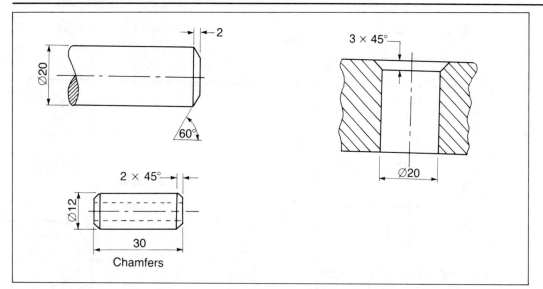

Chamfers

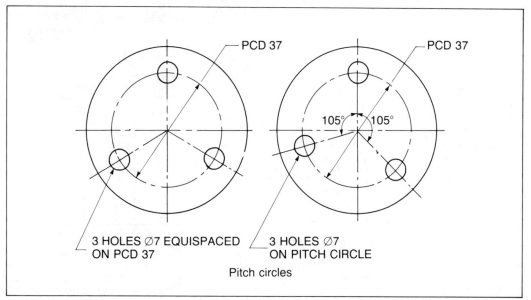

3 HOLES Ø7 EQUISPACED
ON PCD 37

3 HOLES Ø7
ON PITCH CIRCLE

Pitch circles

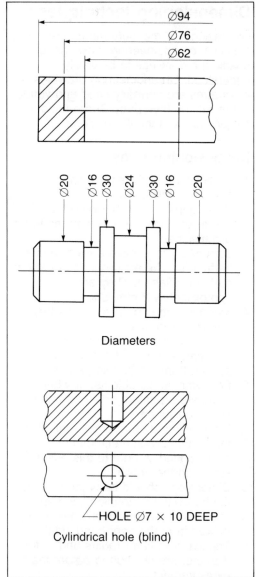

Diameters

HOLE Ø7 × 10 DEEP

Cylindrical hole (blind)

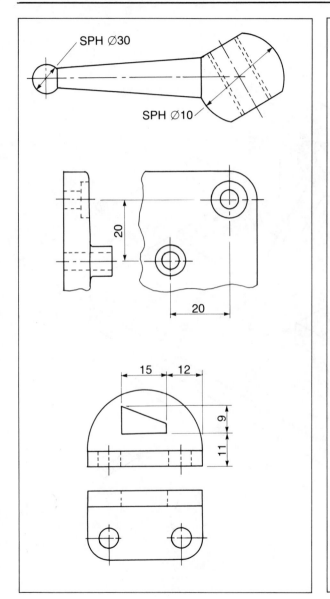

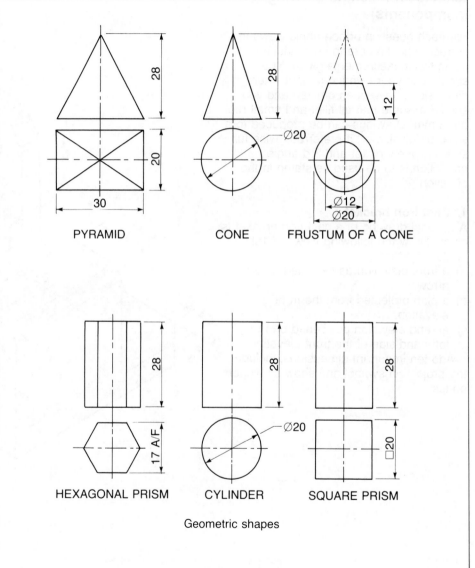

PYRAMID   CONE   FRUSTUM OF A CONE

HEXAGONAL PRISM   CYLINDER   SQUARE PRISM

Geometric shapes

Exercises: machine drawing (components)

For each question orthographic views in correct projection are to be produced using the measurements given. You should use your own judgement where dimensions have been omitted and you should assume that all fillet and small radii are 3 mm. Drawings can be produced to a scale of full size or, if preferred, twice full size. A variety of 1st and 3rd angle projection is to be used as stated in the question.

1. Cast iron bracket

A pictorial drawing of a cast iron bracket is given. Draw the following views in 1st angle projection:
a) a front elevation as indicated by the arrow,
b) a plan projected from the front elevation,
c) an end elevation positioned on the left-hand side of the front elevation.

Add ten important dimensions, include the projection symbol and show all hidden edges.

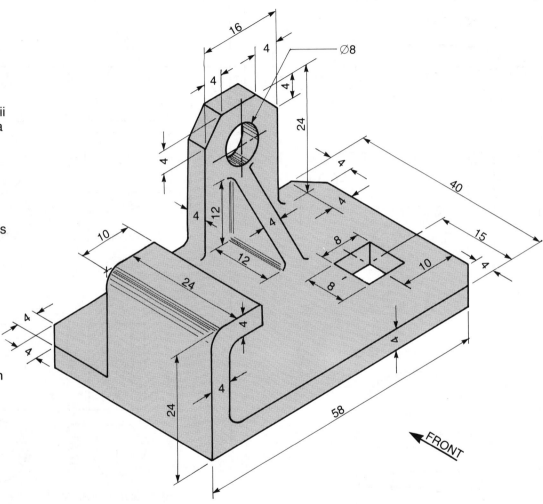

2. Drilling jig

Using the information given on the pictorial drawing of a drilling jig, draw the following views in 1st angle projection. Show all hidden edges:

a) a front elevation looking in the direction of the arrow,

b) a plan projected from the front elevation,

c) an end elevation positioned on the right-hand side of the front elevation.

Insert ten important dimensions on your drawing.

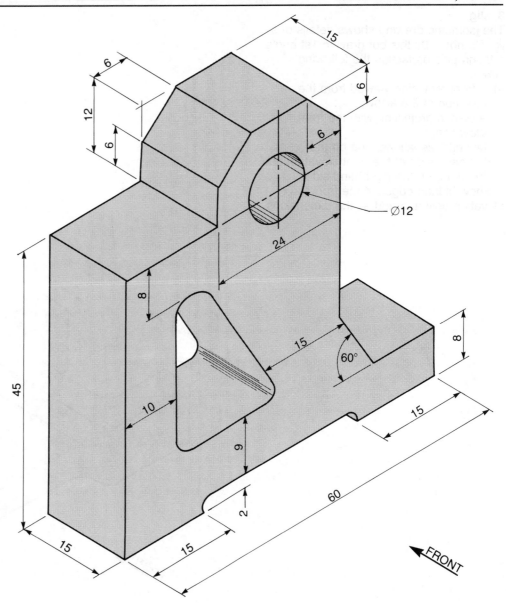

3. Jig

The isometric drawing shows details of a jig. Do not copy this but draw in 1st angle orthographic projection the following views:

a) a front elevation viewed from the direction of the arrow,
b) a plan in projection with the front elevation,
c) two end elevations, one on the left-hand side of the front elevation and the other on the right-hand side.

Show hidden edges in the front elevation only and add all the dimensions.

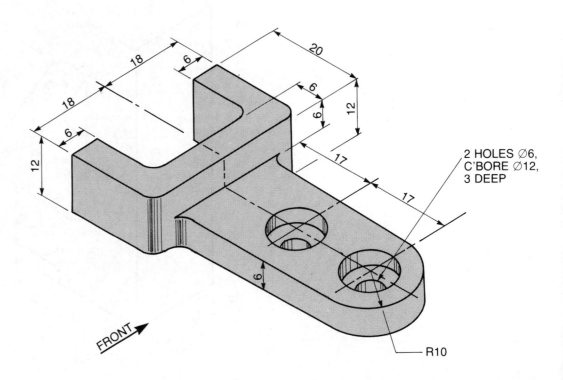

2 HOLES Ø6,
C'BORE Ø12,
3 DEEP

FRONT

R10

4. Bolster block

A pictorial view of a bolster block is given. Using the information on the pictorial view, draw the following orthographic views in 3rd angle projection:

a) a front elevation as indicated by the arrow,
b) a plan projected from view a),
c) an end elevation to the left-hand side of the front elevation.

Fully label your drawing including all the dimensions and the projection symbol. All hidden edges should be shown.

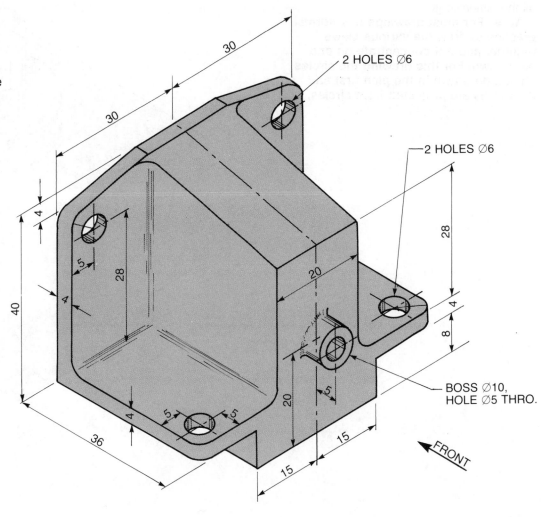

2 HOLES ⌀6

2 HOLES ⌀6

BOSS ⌀10,
HOLE ⌀5 THRO.

FRONT

5. Spigot

Using the pictorial view of the given spigot, draw in 1st angle projection a plan and front elevation only.

Do not show any hidden detail but add all the dimensions.

Note: **For most drawings it is normal practice to draw the various views together and not concentrate on one on its own. For this drawing the circles should be drawn in the plan first and then sizes are projected from circles.**

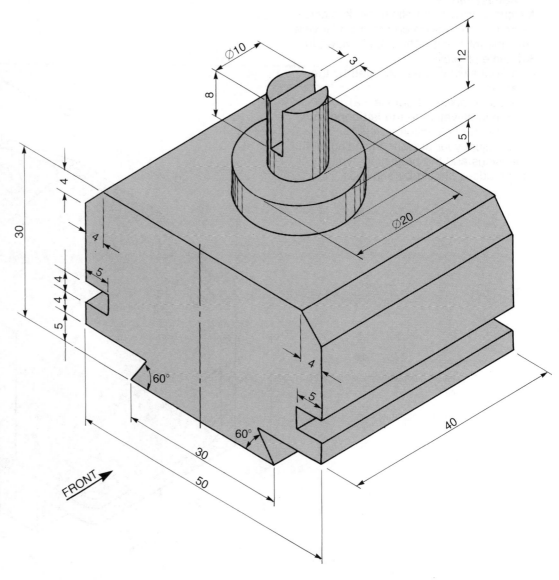

6. Slide block

Using a scale of three times full size, draw the following views of the slide block in 3rd angle orthographic projection:

a) a front elevation viewing it in the direction of the arrow,

b) a plan projected from the front elevation.

c) an end elevation positioned on the left-hand side of the front elevation.

Do not show any hidden edges but add six important dimensions including at least one radius.

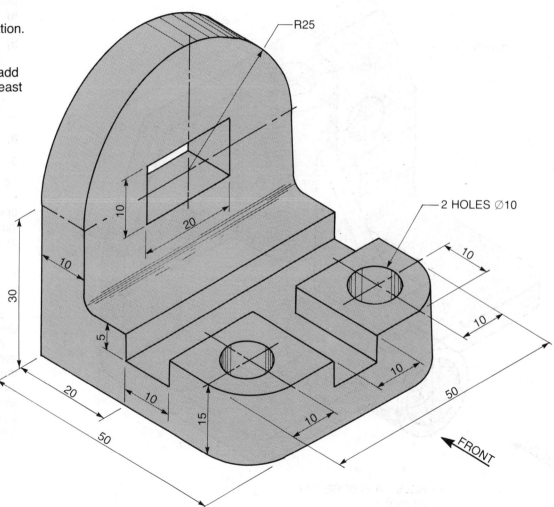

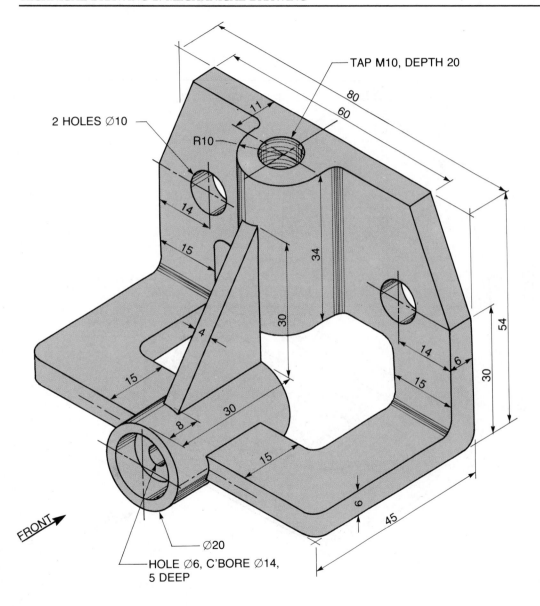

TAP M10, DEPTH 20

2 HOLES Ø10

R10

80

60

11

14

15

4

15

8

30

34

30

14

6

15

54

30

6

45

15

FRONT

Ø20

HOLE Ø6, C'BORE Ø14, 5 DEEP

7. Gear bracket

An isometic drawing of a gear bracket is shown on the left-hand side. Draw the following views in 1st angle orthographic projection:

a) a front elevation in the direction of the arrow,

b) a plan projected from the front elevation,

c) an end elevation positioned on the left-hand side of the front elevation.

Do not show any hidden edges but add all the important dimensions.

8. Bearing

9. Pivot bracket

10. Locating bracket

For each drawing on the opposite page, draw in 3rd angle projection the following views:

a) a front elevation as indicated by the arrow,

b) a plan in projection with the front elevation,

c) an end elevation.

Show all hidden detail and fully dimension each drawing.

Note: Because all three drawings are symmetrical (one half is a mirror image of the other half), dimensions shown on one side will apply to the opposite side. Also assume that all fillet and small radii are 3 mm and that the thickness of all the metal is 5 mm.

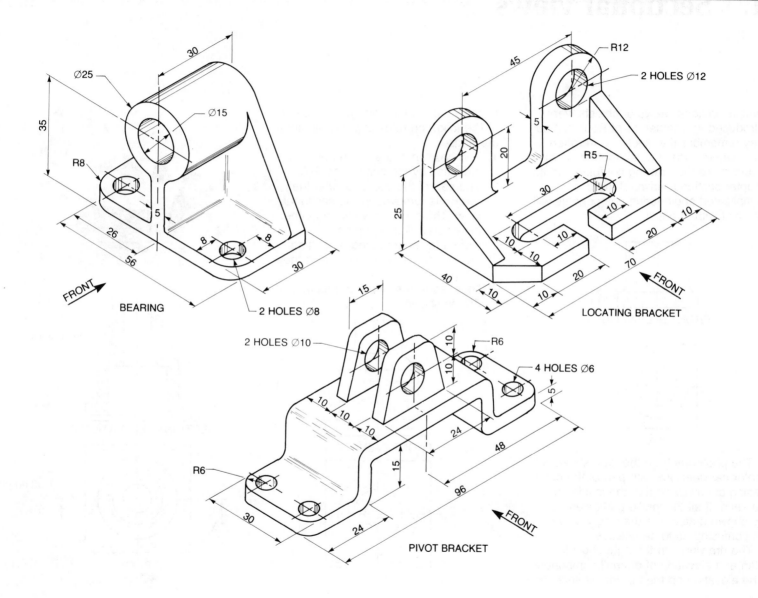

BEARING

Ø25
Ø15
35
30
R8
5
26
56
8
8
30
FRONT
2 HOLES Ø8

LOCATING BRACKET

R12
45
2 HOLES Ø12
5
20
25
R5
30
10
10
10
10
10
10
20
40
10
70
20
FRONT

PIVOT BRACKET

2 HOLES Ø10
15
10
R6
4 HOLES Ø6
10
10
10
10
24
5
48
R6
15
96
30
24
FRONT

4. Sectional views

Simple sectional views of objects were introduced in Chapter 14 of Book 1. You may remember that sections are often used where hidden detail (dotted lines) would make the drawing confusing. In this chapter sectional views of more complicated engineering components will be dealt with in detail.

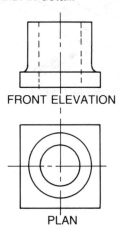

FRONT ELEVATION

PLAN

The photograph on the right shows a motor car gear box with part of the outer casing cut away so that the inside can be seen. If all the inside parts were to be shown dotted, the drawing would be so confusing as to be useless.

The drawings on the right show the plan and elevation of a small component. The elevation on the far right is sectioned

to show the hidden parts more clearly.
The following rules apply to sectional drawings.
1. The position of the cutting plane is indicated by the centre line A-A.
2. The part of the object *behind* the arrows is removed in the sectional view. The sectional view can either be an elevation or a plan.
3. Cut surfaces produced by cutting planes are called sections and they are hatched with thin continuous lines, equally spaced and usually at 45° as shown.

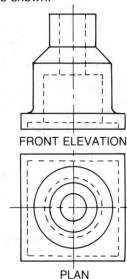

FRONT ELEVATION

PLAN

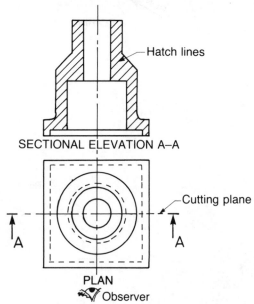

SECTIONAL ELEVATION A–A

Hatch lines

Cutting plane

A   A

PLAN
Observer

Types of sectional views

The conventions and applications of sectional views are shown as follows.

Half sections

For objects that are symmetrical (one half is a mirror image of the other half), it is often convenient to section one half only and to leave the other half as an outside view. Hidden edges can be drawn on the outside view but any hidden detail on the sectional view is omitted. The view is labelled as a half section.

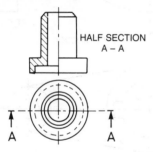

HALF SECTION
A – A

A   A

Local or broken-out sections

Sometimes only a small portion of an object needs to be sectioned to expose internal details. No cutting plane is located but the extent of the break is indicated by an irregular line.

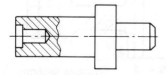

Part or scrap sections

A part or scrap section is similar to a broken-out section except that it is drawn away from the outside view because the view is not suitable for the use of a broken-out section. The cutting plane and line of sight are indicated and the section is labelled as shown.

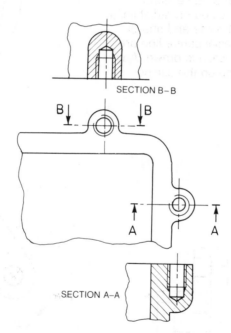

SECTION B–B

B   B

A   A

SECTION A–A

Revolved sections

They are drawn directly on to the outside views to indicate the cross-sections of arms, spokes, rims, etc. The section plane is revolved through 90°.

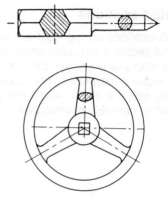

Removed sections

These are similar to revolved sections except that they are not drawn on the outside view.

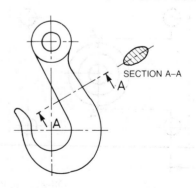

SECTION A–A

A

A

Off-set sections

The illustration below shows an example of an off-set section. The cutting plane is off-set to include features that are not in a straight line. The sectional view is shown as a full section but, where changes of direction take place at right angles, the cutting plane is marked with a heavier line.

Aligned sections

The illustrations on the right are examples of aligned sections. Aligned sections are used when features are located on radial lines. The cutting plane passes through a major centre line and one or more radial centre lines. The features on the radial centre line are aligned with the major centre line before the section is drawn. Any change in direction is indicated by a heavier line on the cutting plane.

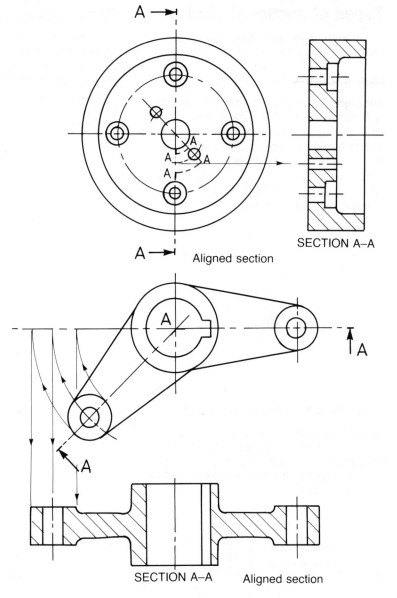

SECTION A–A

Aligned section

SECTION A–A   Aligned section

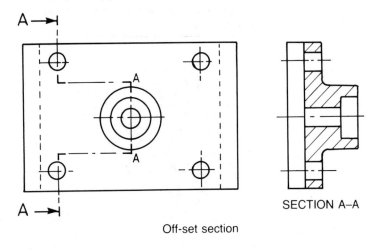

SECTION A–A

Off-set section

Omission of hatch lines

The main purpose of sectioning is to expose the interior of an object when an outside view with hidden detail would be difficult to understand. If hatching certain areas of a sectional view would result in an incorrect interpretation, hatching is omitted. Various rules apply to the omission of hatching as mentioned here.

Webs or ribs

A web or rib is a strengthening or supporting part of a component. In drawing a) the sectional view is incorrect because it gives the impression of the object being solid. When the cutting plane passes through a rib longitudinally b) it is not sectioned. When the cutting plane passes through the rib transversely c) it should be hatched.

Spokes and ribs

The same rules apply to spokes and ribs on wheels as shown opposite.

Details not sectioned on assemblies

The two drawings on page 36 show assemblies of engineering components and you will notice that fixing devices such as nuts, bolts, studs, machine screws and rivets are not sectioned. Also shafts and screw threads are not sectioned. Where there are various different components to an assembly and they are sectioned, the hatching is in different directions and with different spacing for each component so that the components can be easily identified.

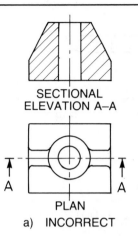

SECTIONAL
ELEVATION A–A

PLAN

a)   INCORRECT

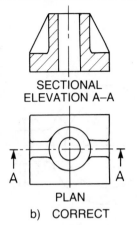

SECTIONAL
ELEVATION A–A

PLAN

b)   CORRECT

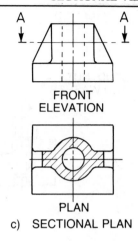

FRONT
ELEVATION

PLAN

c)   SECTIONAL PLAN

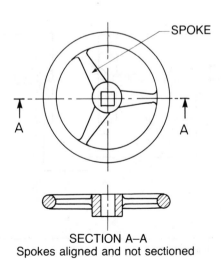

SECTION A–A
Spokes aligned and not sectioned

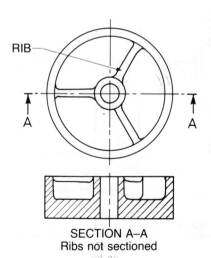

SECTION A–A
Ribs not sectioned

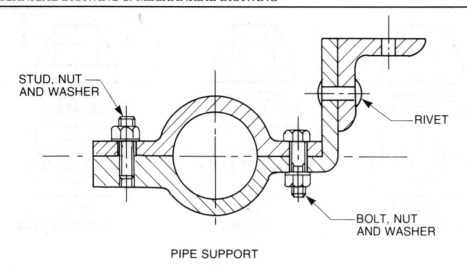

STUD, NUT
AND WASHER

RIVET

BOLT, NUT
AND WASHER

PIPE SUPPORT

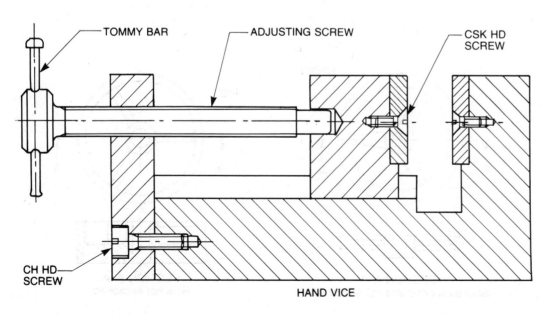

TOMMY BAR

ADJUSTING SCREW

CSK HD
SCREW

CH HD
SCREW

HAND VICE

Understanding sections

The left hand drawing below shows the plan and elevation of a block and the right hand drawing shows the plan and sectioned elevation. The isometric drawing in the lower illustration shows the sectioned block.

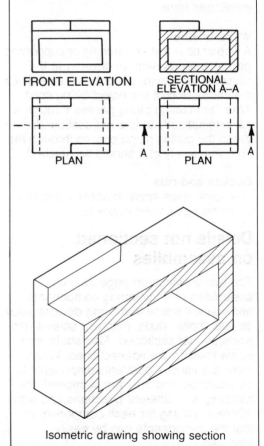

FRONT ELEVATION

SECTIONAL
ELEVATION A–A

PLAN

A

PLAN

A

Isometric drawing showing section

Exercises

For each drawing on this page and overleaf study the views given and produce a freehand sketch in pictorial projection to show the section. Measurements are not given but your sketch should be as large as possible and in good proportion.

All the drawings are in 1st angle projection.

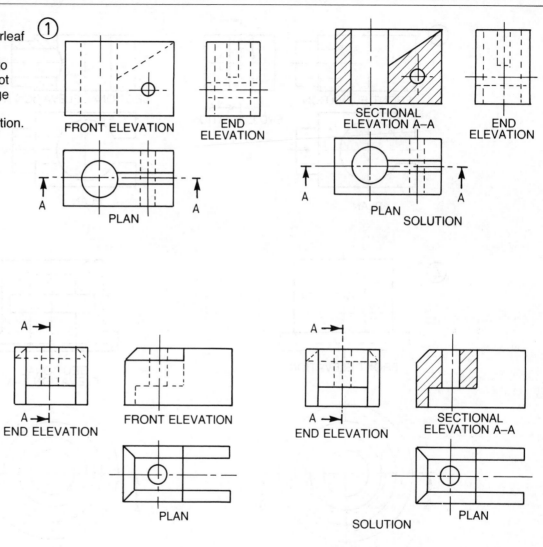

① FRONT ELEVATION   END ELEVATION   PLAN

SECTIONAL ELEVATION A–A   END ELEVATION   PLAN   SOLUTION

② END ELEVATION   FRONT ELEVATION   PLAN

END ELEVATION   SECTIONAL ELEVATION A–A   SOLUTION   PLAN

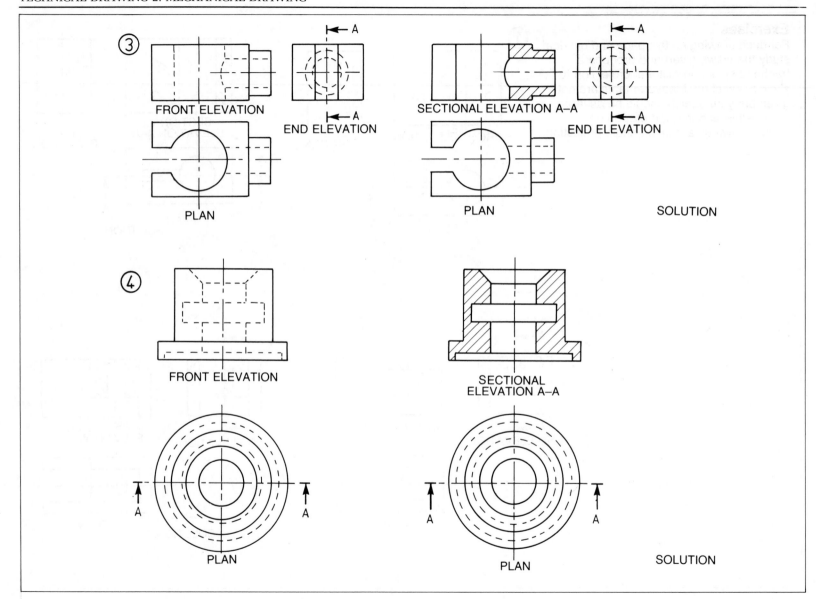

③

FRONT ELEVATION

END ELEVATION

PLAN

SECTIONAL ELEVATION A–A

END ELEVATION

PLAN

SOLUTION

④

FRONT ELEVATION

PLAN

SECTIONAL ELEVATION A–A

PLAN

SOLUTION

Exercises: machine drawing (components)

For each question orthographic views are to be produced including a sectional view as indicated by the cutting plane.

1. Fulcrum support

The drawing shows two views of a fulcrum support in 1st angle projection. Using 3rd angle projection draw the following views:
a) the given plan,
b) a sectional front elevation on A-A,
c) an end elevation positioned on the left-hand side of the sectional front elevation.

Use a scale of full size and insert six important dimensions on the end elevation. Print a title block and include the projection symbol for 3rd angle projection. Assume all fillet and small radii to be 3 mm.

2. Rod bearing

Two views of a rod bearing are given in 3rd angle projection. To a scale of twice full size and in 1st angle projection, draw the following views:
a) the given end elevation,
b) a new front elevation in the direction of arrow A,
c) a plan projected from the new front elevation.

Do not add any dimensions to your drawing. Assume all fillet and small radii to be 3 mm.

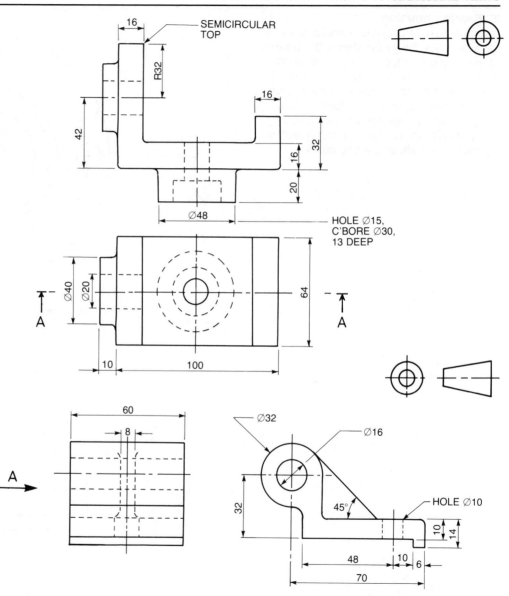

39

3. Bearing housing

Using 3rd angle projection and a scale of full size, draw the given plan of the bearing housing and replace the front elevation with a half sectional elevation on X-X. The right-hand half should be in section and show hidden edges in the outside view.

Do not dimension the drawing but remember to insert the correct projection symbol, all labels and a title block.

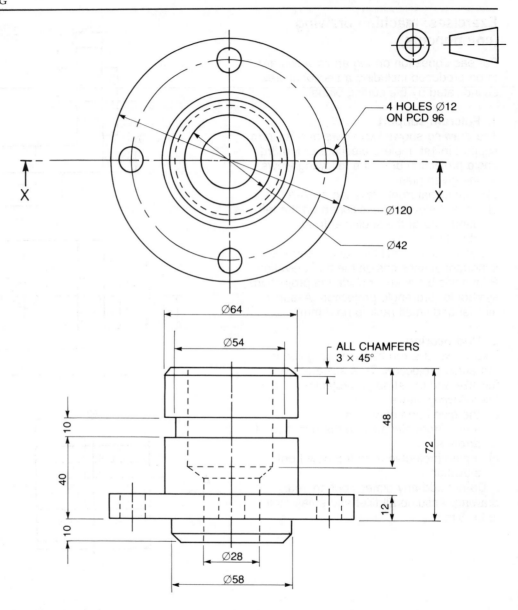

4 HOLES Ø12
ON PCD 96

Ø120

Ø42

X

X

Ø64

Ø54

ALL CHAMFERS
3 × 45°

48

72

10

40

10

12

Ø28

Ø58

4. Housing cover

The drawing shows two views of a housing cover in 3rd angle projection. To a scale of twice full size draw the following views in 1st angle orthographic projection:
a) the given front elevation,
b) a new sectional end elevation on cutting plane B-B,
c) a plan projected from the front elevation.
  Assume all fillet and small radii to be 3 mm. Add all the dimensions to your drawing.

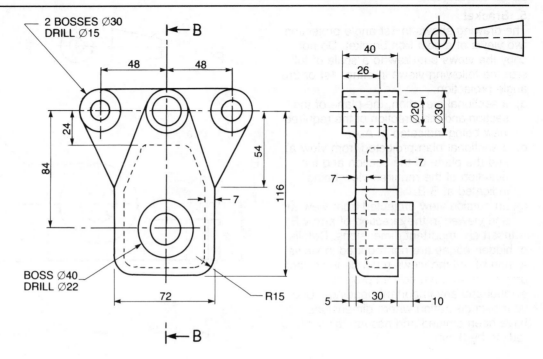

2 BOSSES ⌀30
DRILL ⌀15

BOSS ⌀40
DRILL ⌀22

48   48

24

84

54

116

7

72

R15

B

B

40

26

⌀20

⌀30

7

7

5   30   10

5. Bracket

The drawing shows in 1st angle projection two views of a cast iron bracket. Do not copy the views but draw to a scale of full size the following views in either 1st or 3rd angle projection:

a) a sectional elevation, the plane of the section and the direction of the required view being indicated at A-A,

b) a sectional plan projected from view a), and the plane of the section and the direction of the required view being indicated at B-B,

c) an outside view projected from view a) and viewed in the direction of arrow E.

Insert six important dimensions. Details of hidden edges are not required in views a) and b). All the views must be in correct projection. Add the correct projection symbol and any important headings. Use your own discretion where dimensions have been omitted and assume all fillet radii to be 3 mm.

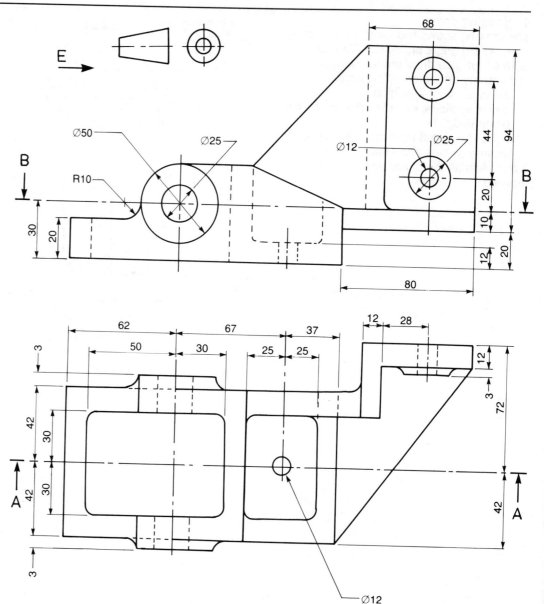

42

6. Gear bracket

Two views of a cast iron gear bracket are given. Do not copy the views but draw full size, in either 1st or 3rd angle projection, the following views:

a) a sectional end elevation, the staggered section planes and the direction of the required view being indicated at A-A,

b) a complete elevation projected from view a) and as seen in the direction of arrow E,

c) a complete plan projected from view b).

Hidden edges are not required on view a). Use your own discretion where dimensions are not indicated and assume all fillet radii are 3 mm. Insert two important dimensions on each view.

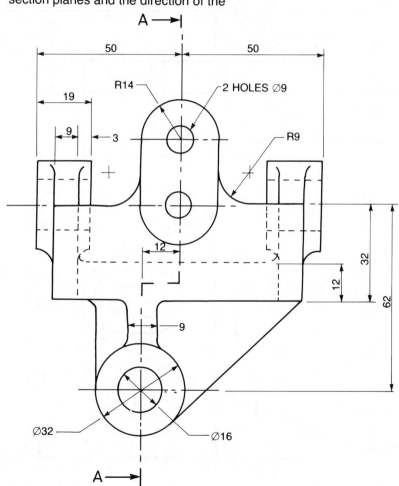

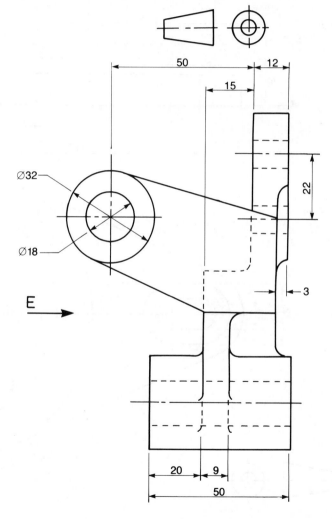

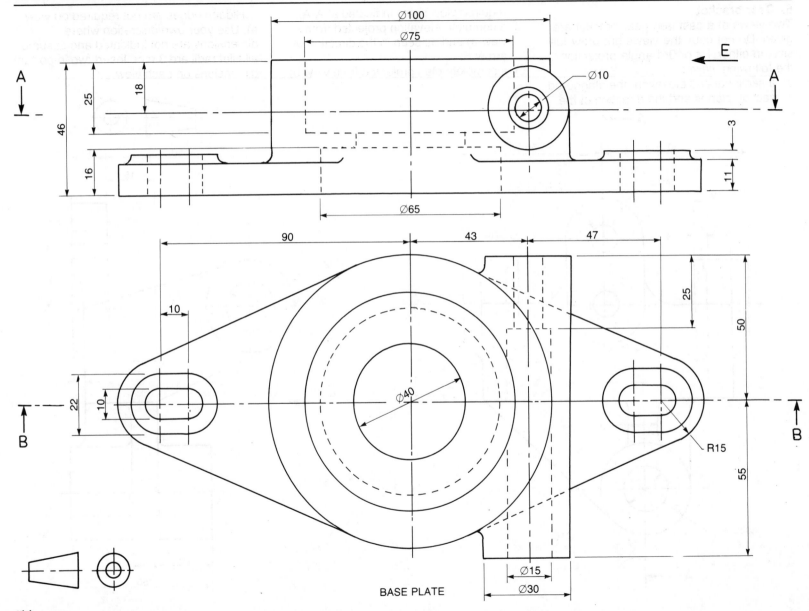

BASE PLATE

7. Base plate

Two views of a base plate in 1st angle projection are given on page 44. Do not copy the views but draw full size the following views in either 1st or 3rd angle projection:

a) a sectional plan, the plane of the section and the direction of the required view being indicated at A-A,

b) a sectional elevation, the plane of the section and the direction of the required view being indicated at B-B,

c) an outside view as seen in the direction of the arrow E.

Use your own discretion where dimensions have been omitted and assume all fillet radii are 3 mm. Insert six important dimensions on your drawing and show hidden edges in view c) only.

8. Pulley coupling

Two views of a pulley coupling are given below. Do not copy these views but draw the following to a scale of full size in either 1st or 3rd angle projection:

a) a new sectional front elevation on B-B,

b) a new sectional end elevation on A-A.

Use your own discretion where dimensions are not given and assume any fillet radii are 3 mm. Do not show any hidden edges or dimensions.

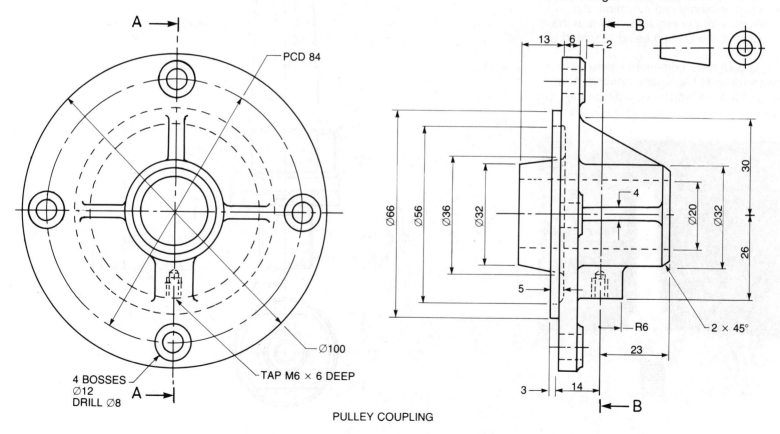

PULLEY COUPLING

9. Chuck

The photograph and orthographic drawings show a chuck for holding milling tools on a vertical milling machine.

Make a freehand pictorial sketch of the chuck and milling cutter as shown in the photograph.

To a scale of full size draw the following views in either 1st or 3rd angle orthographic projection:

a) the given front elevation and plan,

b) a half sectional end elevation, the direction of the required view and the plane of the section being indicated at X-X.

Use your own judgement where measurements have been omitted. Add ten important dimensions, indicate the projection used and include a title block.

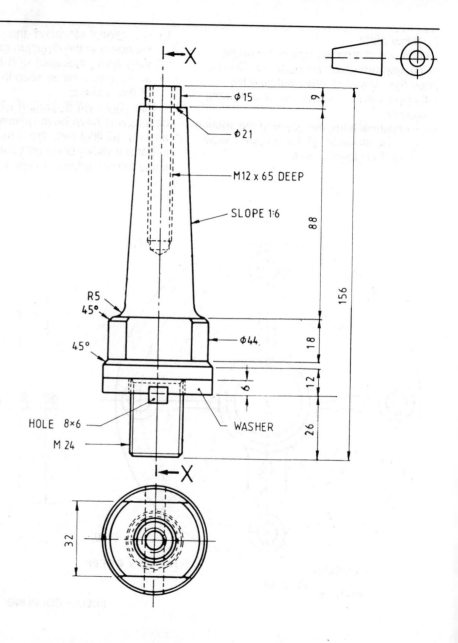

10. Gear box

The drawing shows in 1st angle projection two views of a gear box. Do not copy the views but draw full size, in either 1st or 3rd angle projection, the following views:

a) a sectional elevation, the plane of the section and the direction of the required view being indicated at A-A,

b) an end elevation projected from view a) looking in the direction of arrow C.

Use your discretion for any dimensions not given. Details of hidden edges are not required in view a). Insert six important dimensions on your drawing, include a title block and the projection symbol.

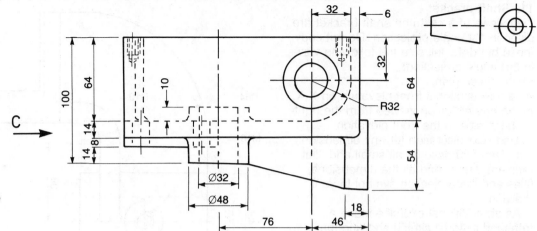

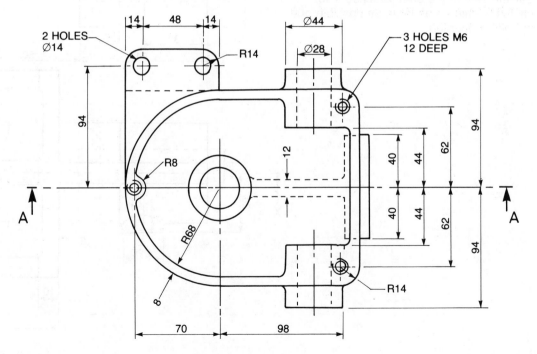

11. Shaft bracket

Two views of a cast iron shaft bracket are given in 1st angle projection. Do not copy these but draw full size the following views in 3rd angle projection:

a) the given plan,
b) a new sectional front elevation on X-X,
c) an end elevation viewed from the right-hand side of the front elevation.

Use your discretion for any dimensions not given and assume all small and fillet radii are 3 mm. Add all the dimensions, titles and the projection symbol to your drawing.

As an additional exercise make a freehand pictorial sketch showing the outside only of the shaft bracket. Your sketch should be as large as possible and in good proportion.

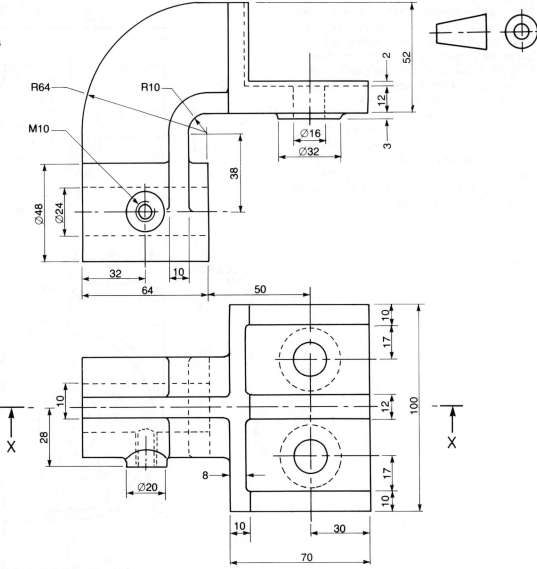

12. Anchor block

The drawing shows two views of a cast iron anchor block. Do not copy the views but draw full size, in either 1st or 3rd angle projection, the following:

a) a sectional elevation, the section plane and the direction of the required view being indicated at X-X,

b) a sectional plan projected from view a), and the plane of the section and the direction of the required view being indicated at X-X,

c) an outside end elevation projected from view a) and as seen in the direction of arrow E.

All fillet and small radii are 3 mm. On each of the three views insert two important dimensions. Hidden detail is not required.

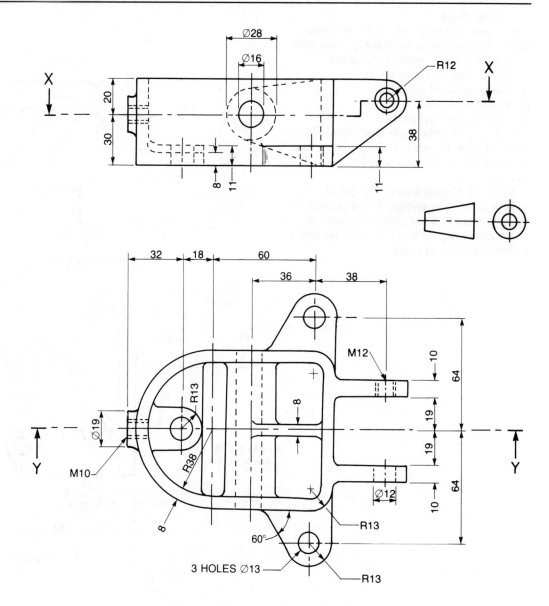

49

13. Base block

The drawing shows two views of a base block in 3rd angle orthographic projection. To a scale of 1:1, draw in 1st angle projection the following views:
a) the given front elevation,
b) a sectional view on A-A,
c) a sectional view on B-B.

All fillet and small radii are 3 mm. Do not show any hidden edges. On views b) and c) dimension two holes and two overall lengths.

As an additional exercise make a freehand pictorial sketch of the outside of the base block. Your sketch should be approximately to a scale of full size and it should be in good proportion.

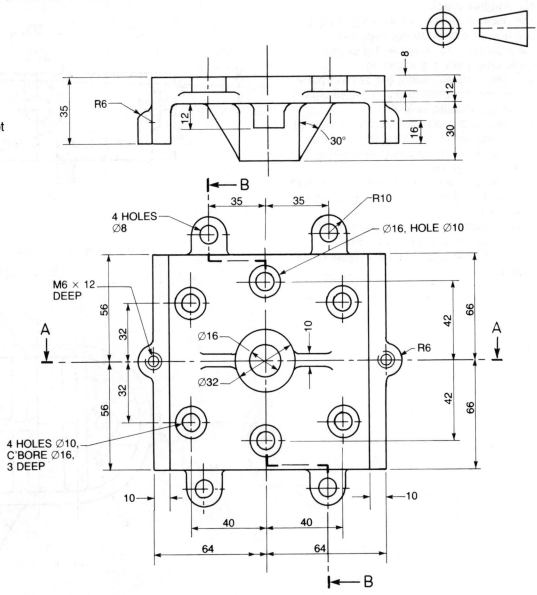

14. Valve body

The diagram shows two views of a valve body drawn in 1st angle projection. To a scale of full size, draw the following views in 1st angle projection:

a) the given plan,

b) a sectional elevation, the plane of the section and the direction of the required view being indicated at X-X,

c) an end elevation projected from the view drawn in b) as seen in the direction of arrow E.

Use your own judgement where dimensions are not given and assume any fillet and small radii are 3 mm. Show hidden edges in views a) and c) only. Indicate on your drawing the following dimensions: overall height, width, a diameter, a fillet radius, a tapped hole and an angle.

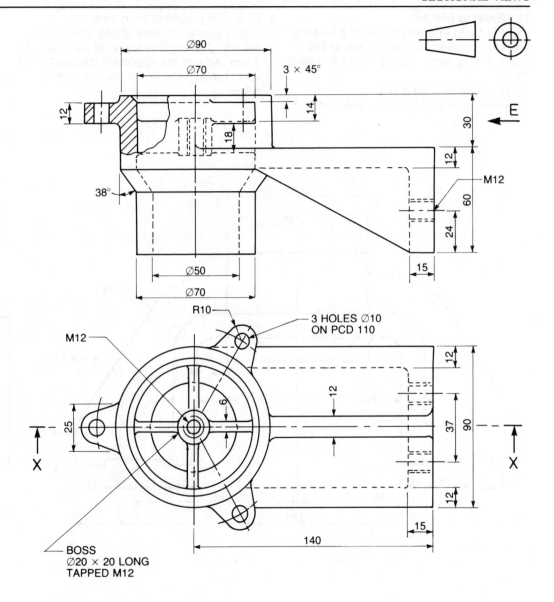

15. Bearing bracket

The front and end elevations of a bearing bracket are given. Draw full size in 3rd angle orthographic projection the following views:

a) the given end elevation,
b) a new sectional front elevation on X-X,
c) a plan projected from view b).

Use your discretion where dimensions are not given and assume all fillet radii are 3 mm. Add all the important dimensions to your drawing. Do not show any hidden edges.

As an additional exercise make a freehand pictorial sketch of the bearing bracket. Your sketch should be approximately full size and it should be drawn in good proportion. Position your sketch to show as much detail as possible.

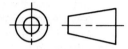

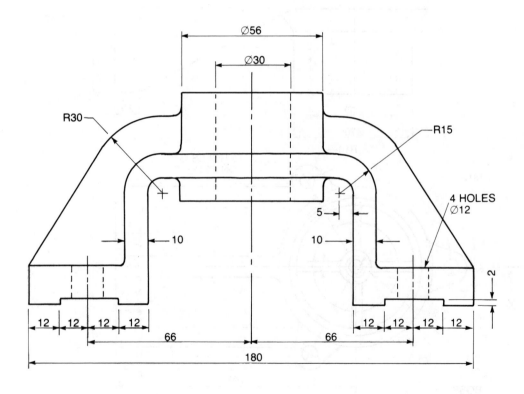

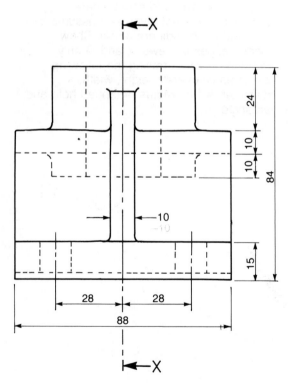

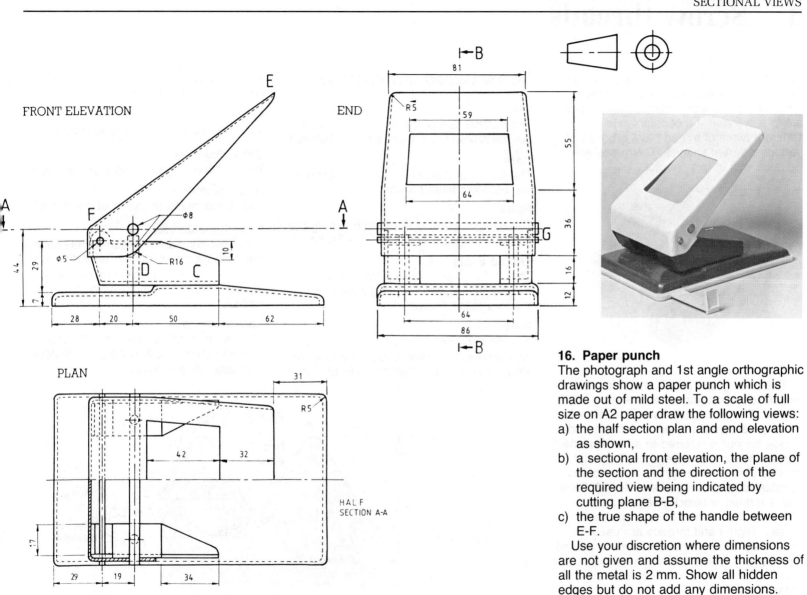

FRONT ELEVATION

E

A

F

Φ8

Φ5

R16

D   C

10

44   29   7

28   20   50   62

PLAN

31

R5

42   32

HALF
SECTION A-A

17

29   19   34

END

B

81

R5

59

55

64

A

G

36

16

12

64

86

B

16. Paper punch
The photograph and 1st angle orthographic drawings show a paper punch which is made out of mild steel. To a scale of full size on A2 paper draw the following views:
a) the half section plan and end elevation as shown,
b) a sectional front elevation, the plane of the section and the direction of the required view being indicated by cutting plane B-B,
c) the true shape of the handle between E-F.

Use your discretion where dimensions are not given and assume the thickness of all the metal is 2 mm. Show all hidden edges but do not add any dimensions.

5. Screw threads

The helix (see Chapter 20 of Book 1) is the basis of all screw threads. It is the locus of a point which moves around and along a cylinder at a constant rate. Different types of thread have grooves of various different shapes. Their uses will be dealt with in this chapter.

The photograph above shows a nut and bolt which is a common engineering fixing device. The thread on the bolt is referred to as an **external thread** and the thread inside the nut is referred to as an **internal thread**. When viewed end on, if the nut is rotated clockwise to tighten it, the thread is referred to as a right-hand thread. If the nut is rotated anticlockwise to tighten it, the thread is referred to as a left-hand thread. Right-hand threads are used for most purposes; left-hand threads are used in situations where the nut may undo, such as for holding a pulley on to a rotating shaft.

Screw thread terminology

Crest
The outside part of the thread. The term applies to both internal and external threads.

Root
The lowest portion of the groove between two adjacent thread forms.

Flank
The straight sides of the thread joining the root and the crest are called the flanks.

Thread angle
This is the angle between the flanks measured in a plane which passes through the axis of the screw.

Pitch
The distance between two adjacent crests on a thread. The pitch equals the *lead* for single start threads, half the lead for two start threads, a third of the lead for three start threads and so on.

Lead
Axial distance moved for one revolution.

Major diameter
This is the outside diameter of the thread.

Minor diameter
This is the inside diameter of the thread.

Effective diameter
The effective diameter, sometimes called the pitch diameter, is the major diameter minus the pitch. This is the diameter that is used when calculating stress in a thread.

Thread depth
The thread depth is half the difference between the major and minor diameters (the depth of a groove).

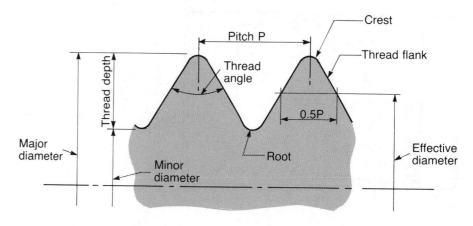

Representing screw threads

Drawing the helix in the photograph of a nut and bolt would be very time consuming. Screw threads are therefore represented by the conventions shown in these drawings.

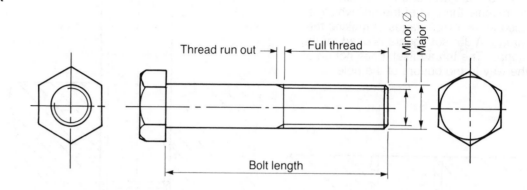

Thread run out → | → Full thread ← | Minor ⌀ Major ⌀

Bolt length

Hexagon headed bolt

The drawing shows the front elevation and two end elevations in 1st angle projection. Note the following rules.
1. The major diameter is shown as a thick line and the minor diameter is shown as a thinner line.
2. A thick line is drawn at the end of the thread with run outs at 30°.
3. In the end elevation (left) the major diameter is shown as a full circle and a thick line. The minor diameter is shown as a thinner line which is broken between centre lines.

Internal thread

The drawing shows the elevation and a sectional elevation A–A of an internal thread. The following rules apply to internal threads.
1. The minor diameter is drawn as a thick line and the circle is complete.
2. The major diameter is drawn as a thinner line and the circle is broken between centre lines.
3. In sectional views hatching lines are drawn across the thread when it is *not* in contact with an external thread such as a bolt.

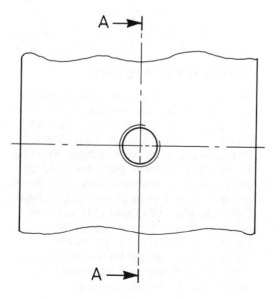

A→

A→

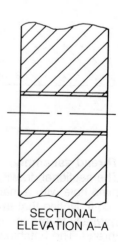

SECTIONAL
ELEVATION A–A

Tapped blind hole

The conical lower end of the hole represents the end of the drill which is used in the initial stages of making the thread. A 30° set square is used for the slopes. The thread itself does not go all the way to the bottom of the hole.

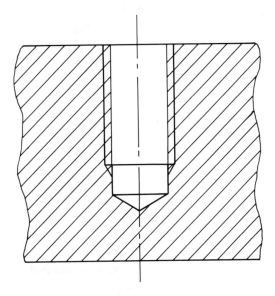

Thread assembly

The sectional drawing shows a tapped blind hole with a machine screw fixed into it. Notice that the screw does not normally fit into the total depth of the thread. The hatching lines do not cover the threaded area.

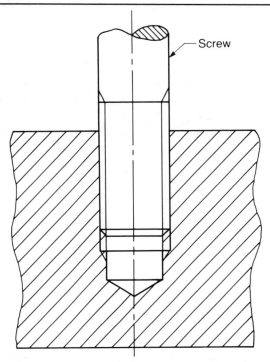

Screw

Screw thread forms

The vee form thread is the most common for fastening devices. Various types of vee form thread exist for different purposes. Some threads are coarser than others and have a greater pitch; screws with fine threads and a smaller pitch are used for electrical and instrument work. As a result of metrication, thread forms such as BSW, BSP, BA, BSF, UNC and UNF are now obsolete. These threads were based on the imperial system of units (inches). Because they can still be found in various items of machinery and equipment, a knowledge of them is necessary.

British Standard Whitworth (BSW)

The BSW thread is a coarse thread. The thread angle is 55° and the crest and root radii are the same. The British Standard Fine (BSF) thread has the same symmetrical cross-section but the pitch is less. The British Standard Pipe (BSP) thread is similar and is used for pipes.

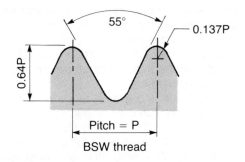

BSW thread

British Association (BA)

The BA thread is a symmetrical vee form with a thread angle of 47½°. It is used in the electrical and electronic industries because of its smallness and very fine pitch.

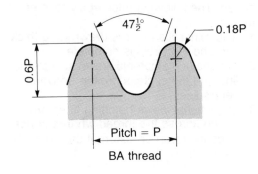

BA thread

Unified thread

Unified coarse (UNC) and unified fine (UNF) threads also have a symmetrical vee form and have a thread angle of 60°. The crests and roots are normally flat but sometimes they can be radiused. Unified threads were common in the motor industry.

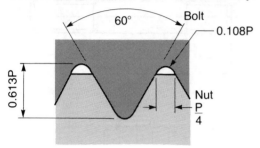

The ISO-metric thread is similar to the unified thread in form. The crests and roots are often flat and the corners can be slightly radiused. The main difference between the metric thread and the unified thread is that the diameters for metric threads are based on millimetres whereas the unified thread diameters are based on fractions of an inch.

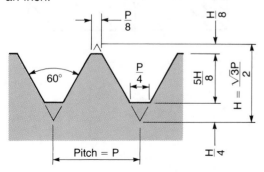

Procedure for drawing a hexagon nut

All the measurements are based on the major diameter (D) of the thread.

Stage 1 The *plan* is drawn first. Using a diameter of 1.5D draw the circle for the chamfer and construct a regular hexagon around it.

From the plan project the corners of the hexagon into the *front elevation*. Show the thickness of the nut as 0.8D and draw the chamfer curves as shown. R is half the distance across the flats of the hexagon.

On the *end elevation* draw the chamfer curves as shown.

Stage 2 Draw the chamfer curves on the second face. On the bolt head only one face is chamfered.

Stage 3 Draw 30° chamfers tangential to the curves in the front elevation and thicken the outlines.

Note: The procedure for drawing the hexagon nut and bolt is quite time consuming. In practice experienced draughtsmen tend to estimate the curves and sizes once the plan (hexagon) has been drawn. An alternative is to use a special template or dry transfer sheets of nuts and bolts.

1.

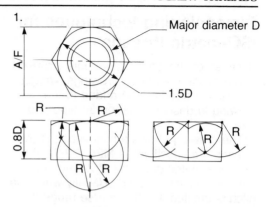

2.

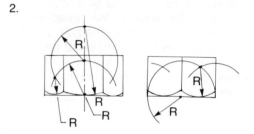

3.

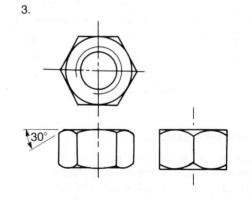

Dimensioning techniques for ISO-metric threads

Because conventions or symbols are used to represent threads on drawings, written information needs to be added to the drawing to describe the thread type and size.

The drawing shows a typical bolt. The threads are specified as M24 X 2. M24 means a metric diameter of 24 mm and 2 means a pitch of 2 mm. Usually when the pitch is omitted it is the coarse range that is specified. For example M24 means M24 × 3. The length of the thread is 50 mm and the length of the bolt is measured from the underside of the hexagon head. Sometimes the dimension to the limit of the thread run out, X, is also given.

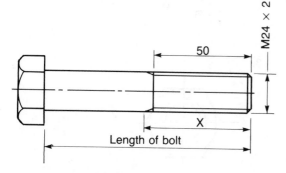

Internal threads

The drawings show the methods of dimensioning internal threads. Normally threads are assumed to be right hand; the abbreviation LH is used for a left hand thread.

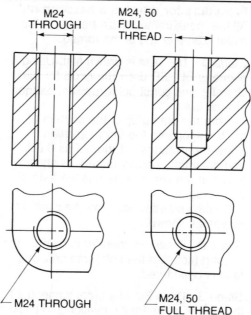

M24 THROUGH

M24, 50 FULL THREAD

Nut and bolt assembly

Note clearance hole and thread run out.

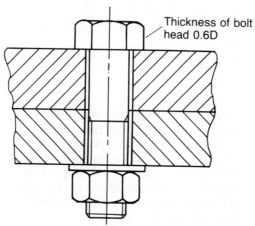

Thickness of bolt head 0.6D

Stud and nut assembly

Note the position of the thread run outs, clearance hole and washer.

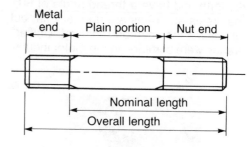

Metal end — Plain portion — Nut end

Nominal length

Overall length

STUD

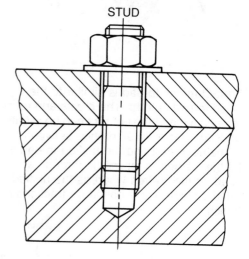

Power thread forms

All three common types of power thread form mentioned here are used for transmitting power between various parts of machinery.

Square thread

The root and crest are both flat and the flanks are normal to the axis. A section through the thread is a square of sides half the pitch. The square thread presents a robust screw for controlled movement in machine vices, the lead screws of lathes, presses, screw jacks and the spindles of valves.

Size conventions do not apply to square threads.

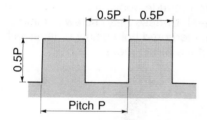

Buttress thread

The buttress thread form is used for transmitting heavy loads in one direction only, as indicated by the arrow. It is used in screw vices such as the woodwork vice shown in the photograph. The flank that transmits the heavy load has an angle of 7° to the vertical, with the thread angle being 52°. The crest is flat and the root is radiused.

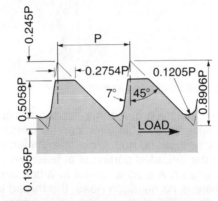

Acme thread

The acme thread is a modified form of square thread. It is easier to machine than a square thread. The depth is the same (one half pitch) and the thickness of the thread measured on the pitch line is also half the pitch. It has a symmetrical vee form of 29° thread angle. It is used for producing transverse motion in machine tools; it is less efficient for load-bearing purposes such as in vertical screw jacks.

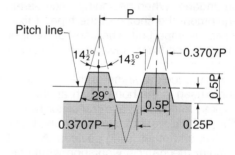

6.   Engineering fasteners

A fastener is any device used for fixing engineering components together. For example a nut and bolt is an example of a temporary method of fixing because the nut and bolt can be undone to dismantle the components. However a permanent method of fixing such as welding cannot be undone. When designing engineering equipment the choice of the type of fixing device is important. The uses of most of the common fixing devices are described in this chapter.

Have a look at some of the common items used in the home such as the cooker, refrigerator and transistor radio. They all use various types of nuts, bolts, screws and other fixing devices. A visit to a motor mechanics' workshop would be an interesting experience. You will see mechanics removing and replacing parts of motor car engines using spanners and screwdrivers to undo and tighten various types of screw, nut and bolt.

Nails and wood screws

Nails and wood screws are used for making temporary joints in timber. Why do you think they are different shapes and sizes?

Bolts and studs

The hexagon nut and bolt is one of the commonest of all engineering fasteners

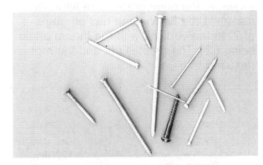
▲ Nails and wood screws

and, because a spanner is used to tighten it up, considerable force can be exerted on the nut and bolt. On a bolt the length of the threaded portion is at least twice the diameter. A stud is similar to a bolt except there is no hexagon head; the thread is on both ends with the centre part unthreaded. Studs are used on motor car engine blocks.

Set screws

Set screws are for lighter work than nuts and bolts. They are tightened up using either a screwdriver, for a slotted head, or a hexagon wrench, for a hexagonal hole in the head.

Countersunk head screws fit into a countersunk hole in the metal and are flush with the surface of the metal. Raised head screws protrude slightly above the surface and are used for instrument work. Round head screws are for general use and protrude above the surface of the metal. Cheese head screws fit into a counterbored hole below or level with the surface of the metal.

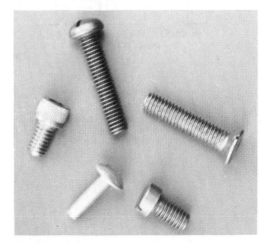

Grub screws

Grub screws have no head and have either a hexagonal hole or a slot. They are often used for locating a pulley on to a shaft, or for other applications where a screw head would be a disadvantage.

Other types of bolt

Nuts and bolts can be made of various metals including steel, brass and aluminium and electroplated with nickel or galvanised with zinc to prevent them rusting.

A coach bolt as shown below is used for joining timber or timber and metal. Notice the square section near the head. This grips into the wood thus preventing the bolt rotating when it is being tightened up.

A tee bolt can be used for fixing a machine vice on to the slotted table of a milling machine.

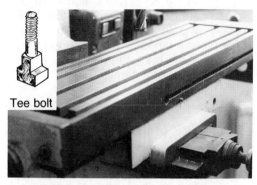

Tee bolt

A rawl bolt (expansion bolt) is for fixing heavy equipment to masonry or concrete.

▲ Rawl bolt

▼ Coach screw

A coach screw is for use in wood. Notice the square section head. The bolt is tightened using a spanner.

An eye bolt has ropes attached to it.

Eye bolt

A U bolt is used for fixing cylindrical material such as pipes to flat objects.

U bolt

The photograph below shows some of the common types of nuts used in engineering. From left to right: square nut, wing nut, castle nut, hexagon nut.

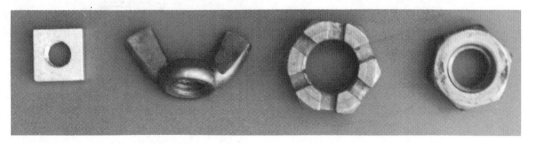

Locking devices

Nuts fitted to machinery which vibrates when operating have a tendency gradually to work loose. To avoid disaster various methods are used to prevent this happening. There are two different types of locking devices: frictional and positive.

Frictional locking devices

Lock nut

This is a second nut which is two thirds the thickness of the normal nut. Both nuts are tightened down. The normal nut on top is then firmly held with a spanner and the lock nut is slightly slackened back against it thus jamming the threads.

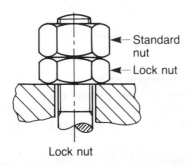

Lock nut

Wiles lock out

The top half of the nut is a clearance hole and, when the set screw is tightened, the threads are caused to jam together. This is only suitable for large nuts. An alternative method is to squash the threads at the end of the bolt with a hammer blow or a centre dot.

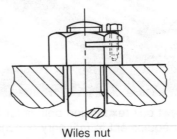

Wiles nut

Stiff (Simmonds) nut

The drawing shows a half section through a stiff (Simmonds) nut. A fibre or nylon insert of a smaller diameter than the major diameter of the thread is fitted inside a groove. When the nut is applied the threads grip into the ring which locks the nut by means of friction.

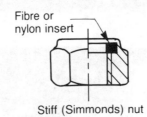

Stiff (Simmonds) nut

Grub screw

The drawing shows a half section throug a circular nut which is locked by a grub screw. The grub screw bears against a brass pad which prevents damage to the bolt threads.

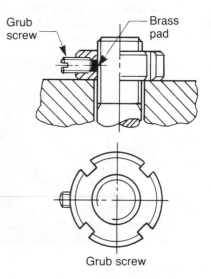

Grub screw

Spring and star washers

The photograph shows different types of spring and star washers which can also be used as frictional locking devices.

▲ Spring washers

▲ Star washers

Positive locking devices

Split pin

The end of the bolt is machined down to a diameter to remove the thread, a small hole is drilled through as shown and a split pin is inserted. The legs of the split pin are bent over the bolt end.

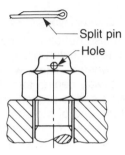

Taper pin

The taper pin is driven through a small hole in both the bolt and the nut. The end of the taper pin is split and opened out to prevent it coming out of the hole.

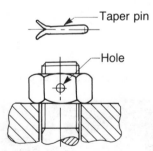

Slotted nut

This is a hexagonal nut with six slots machined across the top surface. A split pin is driven through one slot and a hole in the bolt. The ends are opened out and bent around the faces of the nut.

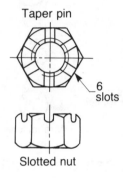

Slotted nut

Castle nut

This is similar to a slotted nut except that there is a cylindrical rim at the top.

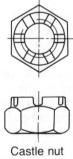

Castle nut

Ring nut

A ring nut is a hexagonal nut with a grooved cylindrical collar on the lower portion into which a set screw fits.

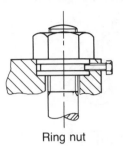

Ring nut

Locking plate

This is a flat plate with a bi-hexagonal hole to locate against the nut. The locking plate is fixed in place by means of a set screw and spring washer.

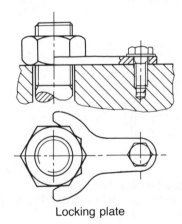

Locking plate

Tab washer

There are two types of tab washer. Both have a leg which is bent against one face of the nut. The leg at the other end can be bent at right angles against the side of the casting or be bent into a drilled hole.

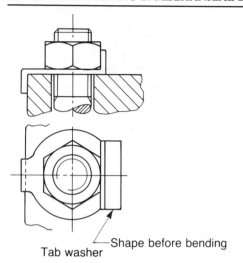

Tab washer

Shape before bending

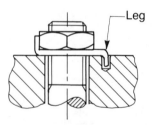

Leg

Siamese tab washer

A Siamese tab washer is used to engage two nuts in one go.

Siamese tab washer

Wire locking

Thin soft wire is passed through holes in two adjacent nuts. The wire is then twisted as shown using pliers.

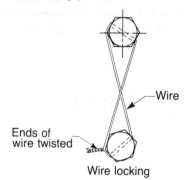

Wire

Ends of wire twisted

Wire locking

Fixing gears and pulleys on to shafts

There are numerous methods of fixing pulleys and gears on to shafts. Two important factors should be taken into account.

1. It is often necessary to remove the pulley from the shaft and therefore any fixing device should not damage the shaft.
2. When fixing gears, to avoid damaging the teeth if the machine jams, the fixing device should act as a 'weak link'. In other words the fixing device will shear and thus the gear teeth will not be damaged.

The photograph of part of a small bandsaw shows the motor pulley fixed by means of a key and keyway. A keyway is a slot cut into both the shaft and the pulley. The key, which is rectangular in this case, is

of a softer material than the shaft. The drawings show some different types of keys.

Rectangular tapered · · · · · · · · Gib head · · · · · · · · · · · Woodruff

Different types of keys

You will also notice that the pulley on the machine is held in place by means of a bolt and washer. There would also be a key and keyway behind this. The bolt and washer are used to prevent the pulley falling off the end of the shaft. It is also important to know the direction of rotation as this will determine whether a left or right hand thread should be used.

Another method is to drill a hole through the pulley and shaft and to use a pin. Different types of pin are shown below.

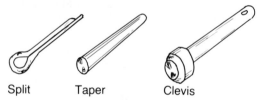

Split · · · · · · · · · Taper · · · · · · · · · Clevis

Different types of pins

The photograph below of part of a lathe shows the gear wheels fixed by means of a set screw which would locate into a groove (or on to a flat) on the shaft. The chuck would be screwed on to the right hand end of the shaft.

Splined shaft

Splined shafts have several slots machined along the length of the shaft. They are used when movement is required along the shaft such as in the steering column of a motor car.

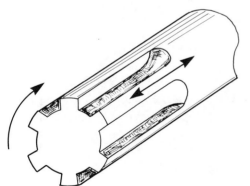

Splined shaft

Serrated shaft

The end is serrated as shown and it is often pushed into a component made of a softer material to give positive contact.

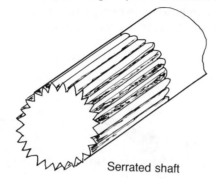

Serrated shaft

Cotter

A cotter is used to join two rods which carry an axial load. One rod end fits into a socket at the end of the other. Both are slotted to take the cotter which is a flat piece of material having a taper at one side.

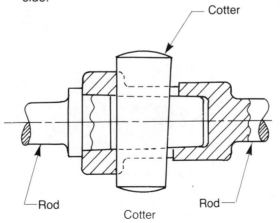

Rod   Cotter   Rod

Cotter pin

This is a cotter with a nut to secure it in position. A cotter pin is used on the crank of a bicycle.

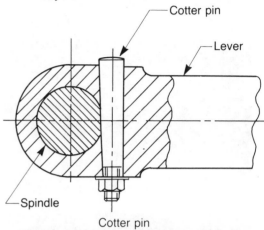

Cotter pin

65

Permanent methods of fixing

Permanent methods of fixing include welding, brazing, soldering, bonding and riveting.

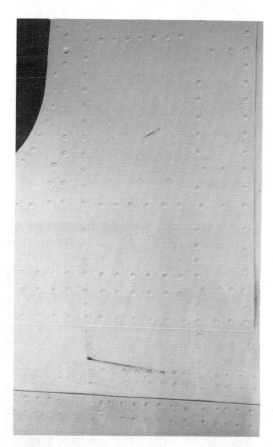

▲ Rivets on an aircraft

Riveting

The drawing shows some of the common rivets used in engineering and different ways of joining sheet metal using rivets. In the ship building industry years ago the hulls of ocean liners were joined together by rivets. However welding is more common today. The lightweight panels on the fuselage and wings of aircraft are still riveted even today. Try to find as many examples of objects that use rivets in their construction.

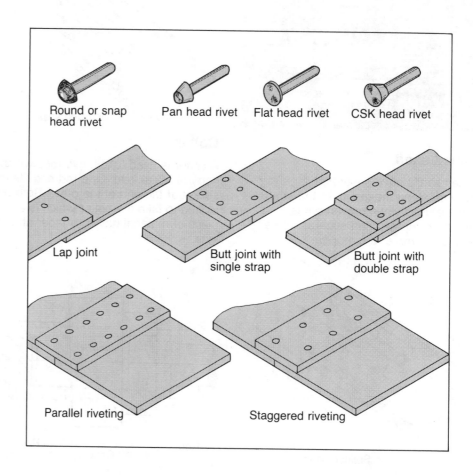

Round or snap head rivet   Pan head rivet   Flat head rivet   CSK head rivet

Lap joint

Butt joint with single strap

Butt joint with double strap

Parallel riveting

Staggered riveting

Welding

Examples of welded joints abound: the body work of motor cars, the burglar bars on windows and doors, many engineering components, the metal legs of tables and chairs, etc. are all welded. Make a list of as many examples as you can find.

The table on the right and the drawings below show the conventions for welded joints on engineering drawings.

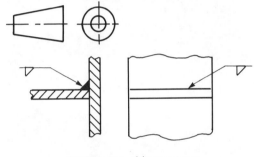

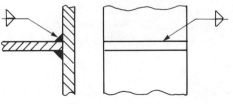

Weld same side as arrow

Weld opposite side from arrow

Weld on both sides

TYPE OF WELD	SECTION	SYMBOL (SINGLE)	SYMBOL (DOUBLE)
Fillet			
Vee butt			
U butt			
J butt			
Square butt			
Bevel butt			
Flush finish (vee)			
Weld all round (fillet)			
Edge			
Spot		(2) 6 3 B Figs. = size, number, pitch	

7. Assembly drawing

It is often convenient to produce separate drawings in orthographic projection of each individual component of a complete engineering object. An assembly drawing has all the individual parts fitted together on one orthographic drawing of the complete object. The various parts are usually fitted together using screws, nuts, bolts and the various fastening devices described in the previous two chapters. Sometimes permanent fixing such as welding or riveting is used.

It can be quite difficult to visualise how each component will fit together and, before starting drawing, a freehand sketch of the possible solution can help. Also matching up measurements such as holes and screw threads can aid working out an assembly problem.

This photograph of a gate valve is an example of a very simple assembly drawing. It shows the top part of the valve screwed into the bottom part. For a complete assembly of the valve all the other parts would also be shown.

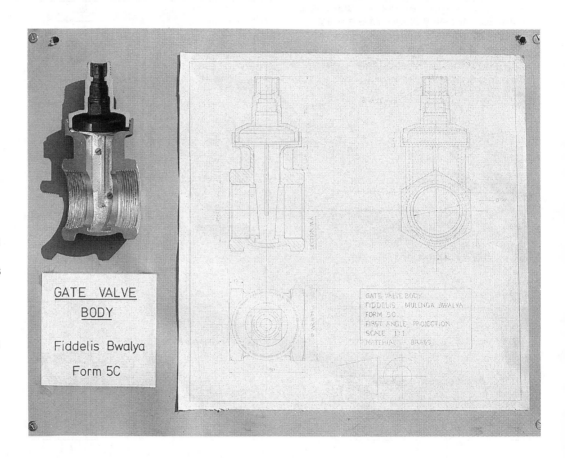

Exercises

Many of these assembly drawing problems have been taken from past examination papers. In each case read the instructions carefully and plan your solution before starting drawing. All dimensions are in millimetres.

1. Flange coupling assembly

The details of a flange coupling assembly are given in lst angle projection. To a scale of twice full size, draw the following views of all the parts completely assembled; also show part of the 12 mm diameter shafts and keys in position:

a) an outside front elevation corresponding to the given elevation of the flange,

b) a sectional end elevation, the plane of the section and the direction of the required view being indicated by cutting plane A-A.

Assume any dimensions not given and that all fillet radii are 3 mm. Do not show any hidden edges or dimensions.

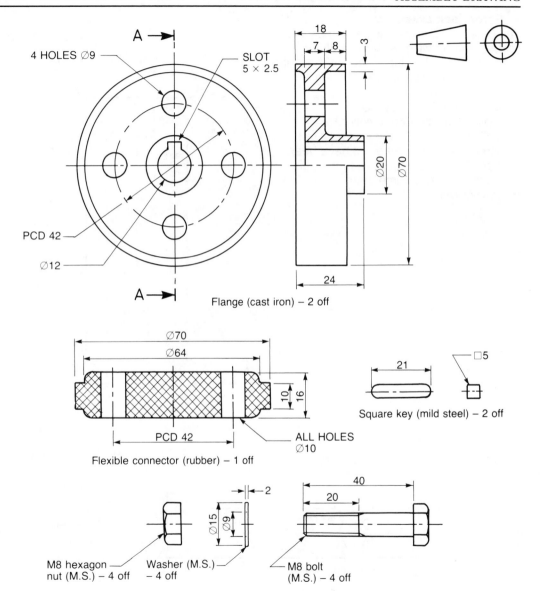

4 HOLES ⌀9
SLOT 5 × 2.5
PCD 42
⌀12

Flange (cast iron) – 2 off

⌀70
⌀64
PCD 42
ALL HOLES ⌀10
Flexible connector (rubber) – 1 off

□5
21
Square key (mild steel) – 2 off

M8 hexagon nut (M.S.) – 4 off
Washer (M.S.) – 4 off
⌀15
⌀9
2
M8 bolt (M.S.) – 4 off
40
20

69

2. Screw jack assembly

The details of a screw jack assembly are given in the drawing. Assemble all the components and, using a scale of half full size, draw the following views using 1st angle projection:

a) a sectional front elevation,
b) a plan projected from view a).

All fillet radii are 3 mm; use your own judgement where dimensions have been omitted. Show hidden edges in the plan only and indicate six important dimensions on your drawing.

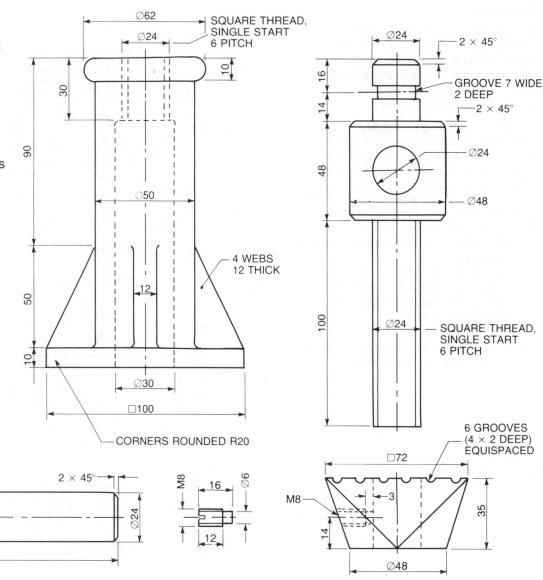

3. Lathe tool holder assembly

The drawing shows the parts of the lathe tool holder in the photograph. With all the parts correctly assembled, draw the following views to a scale of full size:

a) a plan,

b) a sectional front elevation looking in the direction of arrow F, the cutting plane for the section is the centre line passing through the four tapped holes,

c) an end elevation viewed from the left-hand side of the front elevation.

Assume any dimensions not given, add six important dimensions to your drawing and show hidden edges in the plan only.

▲ The assembled lathe tool holder

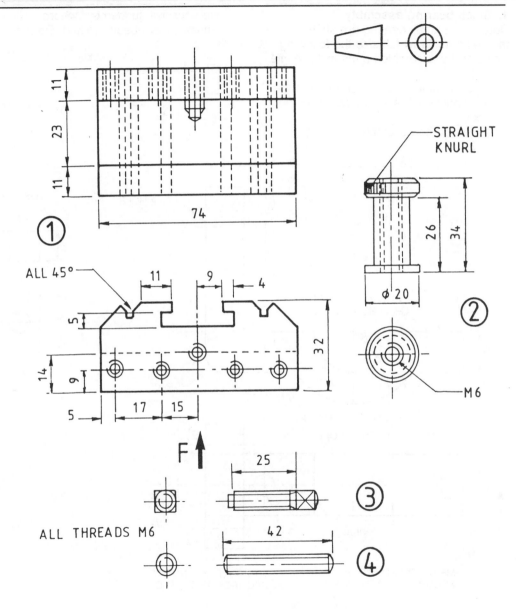

STRAIGHT KNURL

ALL 45°

F

ALL THREADS M6

M6

71

4. Small bearing assembly

Details of a small bearing are shown in the diagram. Draw full size the following views of the assembled parts in 1st angle projection:

a) a sectional front elevation through the assembly on A-A as indicated on the body,

b) a plan of the assembly.

Use your own judgement where dimensions have been omitted. Do not show any hidden edges but insert three important dimensions on each view.

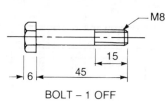

BOLT – 1 OFF

M8 NUT – 2 OFF

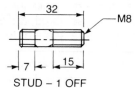

STUD – 1 OFF

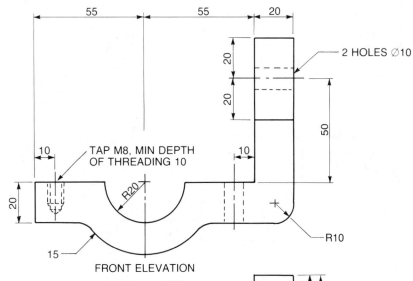

FRONT ELEVATION
BODY – 1 OFF

PLAN

M8 STUD AND NUT TO SECURE CAP TO BODY

Ø10 BOLT AND NUT TO SECURE CAP TO BODY

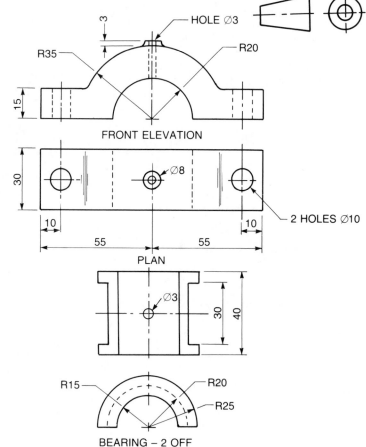

FRONT ELEVATION

PLAN

BEARING – 2 OFF

5. Tool post assembly

The details of a tool post assembly are given in the drawing. To assemble the parts, item 2 is pressed down from the top of item 1 through to the bottom. Item 3 locates above item 2 with a gap of 8 mm between them. Item 4 is located in item 1, resting on item 3, while item 5 locates at the top of item 1.

To a scale of full size in 1st angle projection draw the following:
a) a sectional front elevation of the assembly,
b) an elevation of the left-hand side of a),
c) a plan of the assembly.

Assume any dimensions not given and that all fillet radii are 3 mm. Do not show any hidden edges.

Show the following dimensions on your drawing: a radius, a diameter, a countersunk hole, a threaded hole, a square and an overall height.

As an additional exercise make a freehand pictorial sketch of the complete assembly. Your sketch should be as large as possible and in good proportion.

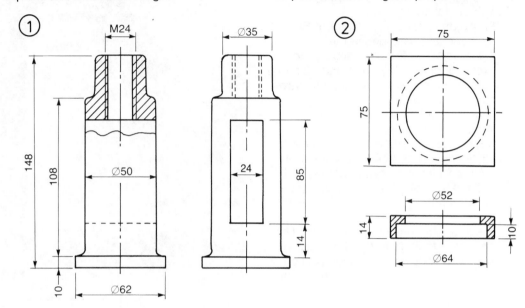

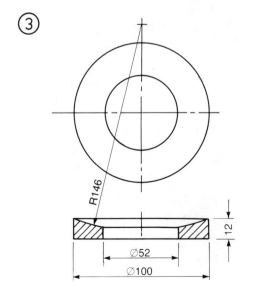

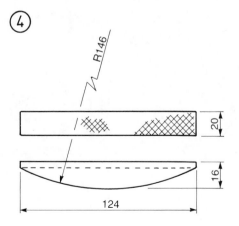

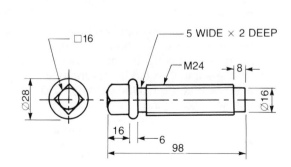

6. Base for office chair assembly

The drawing shows the various parts of the cast aluminium alloy base for the office chair shown in the photograph.

Note the following points.

1. *Pentagon construction*: Refer to Book 1 on plane and solid geometry.
2. *Tangency*: The feet are tangents to two circles of diameter 32 mm and 40 mm. The circles should be accurately drawn but there is no need to use a construction for the straight line tangents joining the circles.
3. *Knob*: The tapped hole at B is for a tightening device which consists of a $\varnothing 8$ rod which is threaded at one end and has a knob at the other end (see photograph).
4. *Break line*: C shows the use of a break line in a tube to shorten the stem. This enables it to fit on to the drawing.
5. *Revolved section*: A revolved section at D shows the cross-sectional shape of the leg at the position where it is drawn.
6. *Spring*: The symbol for a compression spring is shown at E. On a larger drawing the spring (or part of it) could be drawn accurately. Refer to the helix in Chapter 20 of Book 1.
7. Hidden edges for only one leg have been shown. This has been done for the purpose of clarity. Because each leg is the same it would be reasonable to assume that the hidden detail at D is the same for each leg.

To a suitable scale, with one castor in position, draw in 1st angle projection the following views:

a) a plan and elevation as shown,

b) a sectional end elevation, the cutting plane and direction of the required view being indicated at A-A. The castor should be positioned in the leg marked D.

Use your own judgement where dimensions have been omitted. Do not show any dimensions on your drawing but show hidden edges in the plan and front elevation.

As an additional exercise you could show the helical spring as a true helix in the sectional view. The dimensions for the round sectioned spring are as follows; outside diameter 54 mm, cross-section of the spring diameter 6 mm and pitch 36 mm.

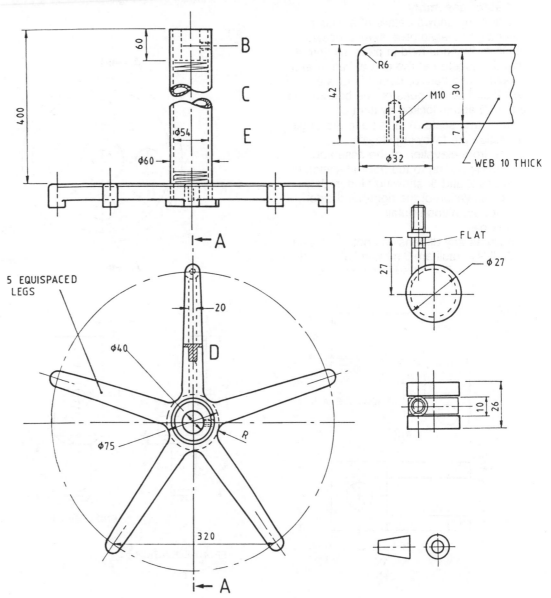

7. Castor assembly

The drawing shows details of a castor assembly. To assemble, item 1 locates into item 2 and is held in place by item 4. Item 5 is located at the end of item 4 and is locked with item 6. Item 3 is located in item 2 and item 5 goes on the bottom end of item 3 and is locked by item 6.

Draw to a scale of full size in 3rd angle projection the following views:

a) the front elevation of the assembly corresponding to the front elevation of items 2 and 3, showing hidden detail,

b) the elevation of the right-hand side, showing hidden detail,

c) the plan.

Assume any dimensions not given and that all fillet radii are 3 mm and all chamfers are 2 × 45°. Do not add any dimensions.

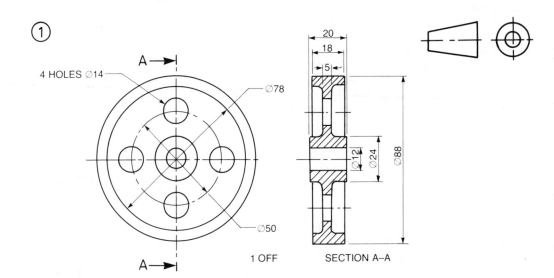

① 4 HOLES ⌀14 ⌀78 ⌀50 1 OFF

SECTION A-A

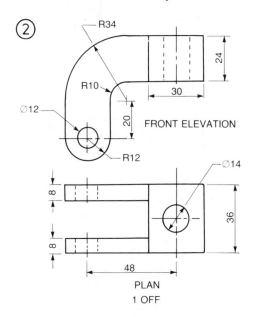

② R34 R10 ⌀12 R12 24 30 20 FRONT ELEVATION

⌀14 8 8 48 36 PLAN 1 OFF

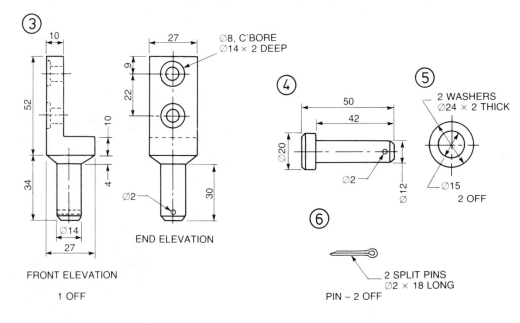

③ 10 52 34 10 4 ⌀14 27 FRONT ELEVATION 1 OFF

27 ⌀8, C'BORE ⌀14 × 2 DEEP 9 22 ⌀2 30 END ELEVATION

④ 50 42 ⌀20 ⌀2

⑤ 2 WASHERS ⌀24 × 2 THICK ⌀12 ⌀15 2 OFF

⑥ 2 SPLIT PINS ⌀2 × 18 LONG PIN – 2 OFF

8. Rotary lever sub-assembly

The diagram shows the component parts for a sub-assembly of a rotary lever which turns with its centre spindle. The lever is shown in 3rd angle projection. Draw full size in 3rd angle projection the following views of the complete assembly:

a) a sectional front elevation on X-X,

b) a complete plan.

All fillet and small radii are 3 mm; use your own judgement where dimensions have been omitted. You are not to show any hidden edges or dimensions on your drawing.

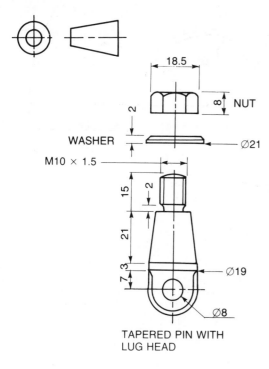

TAPERED PIN WITH LUG HEAD

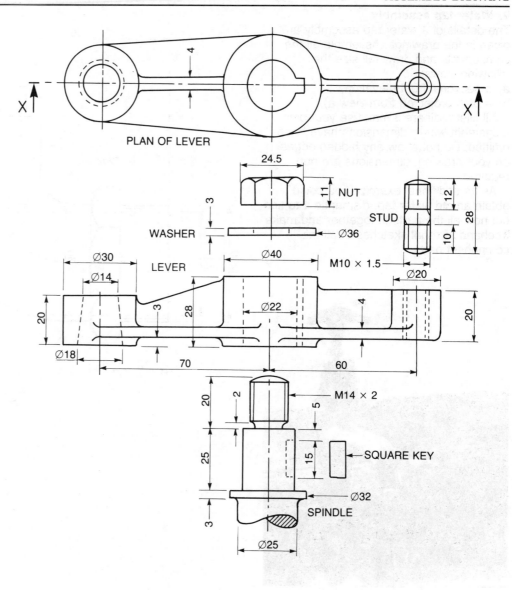

9. Water tap assembly

The details of a water tap assembly are given in the drawings. Assemble all the components and draw full size the following views:

a) a sectional front elevation,
b) a plan projected from view a).

All fillet radii are 3 mm; use your own judgement where dimensions have been omitted. Do not show any hidden edges on your drawing; dimensions are not required.

As an additional exercise you could obtain an old water tap, dismantle it to find out how all the parts fit together and make freehand pictorial sketches of all the component parts.

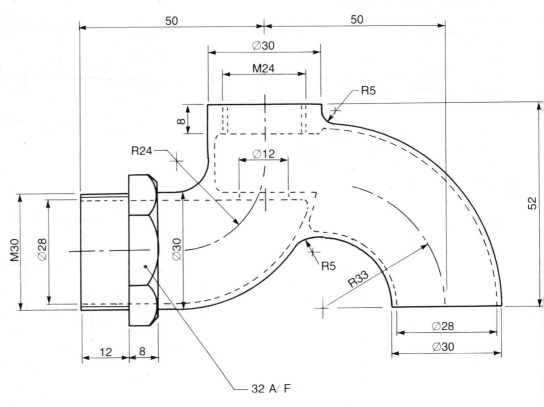

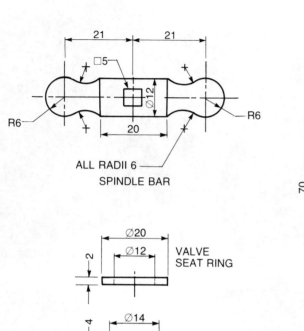

21   21
□5
Ø12
R6   R6
ALL RADII 6
SPINDLE BAR
20

Ø20
Ø12
2
VALVE
SEAT RING

Ø14
4
RUBBER
21   16
Ø4
VALVE

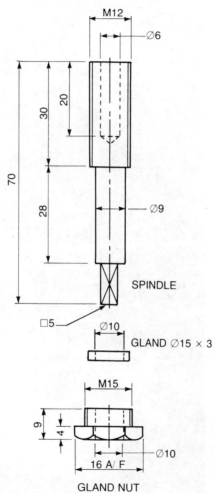

M12
Ø6
20
30
70
28
Ø9
SPINDLE
□5
Ø10
GLAND Ø15 × 3

M15
9   4
Ø10
16 A/F
GLAND NUT

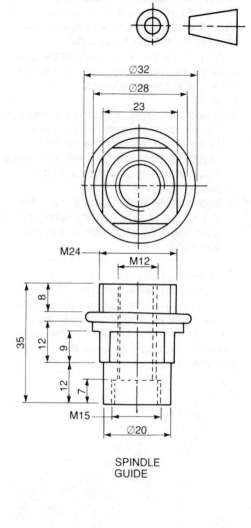

Ø32
Ø28
23

M24
M12
8
35   12   9
12   7
M15
Ø20
SPINDLE
GUIDE

10. Lathe face plate assembly

The photographs and isometric drawing show the component parts of one jaw of a four-jaw face plate for a lathe.

With all the parts correctly assembled, draw in 3rd angle projection to a scale of full size the following views:

a) a plan,

b) a sectional front elevation viewed from the direction of arrow F, the section being taken through the centre of the object (in this view you will only cross-hatch the body and the clamping piece),

c) two end elevations, one viewed from the left-hand side and the other viewed from the right-hand side of the front elevation,

d) a view looking underneath the object (inverted plan) (this view will be positioned *below* the front elevation).

Assume any dimensions not given and do not show any hidden edges. Insert six dimensions; these should be of a varied nature for example a screw thread, diameter, radius, angle, etc.

▶ Four-jaw face plate

▲ The parts of one jaw

▲ The assembled jaw

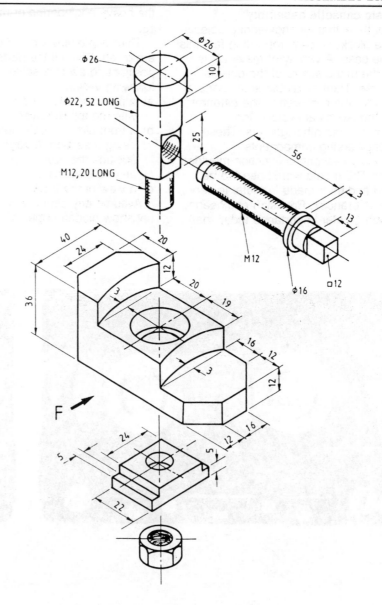

11. Music cassette assembly

You may think that all engineering objects are large blocks of cast iron but in fact this is not the case. A variety of materials is used in the manufacture of the objects that we use. Think of all the small parts of a motor car; the carburettor, the different parts of the electrical system, the speedometer and other gauges. These are all engineering components.

This music cassette is injection-moulded in plastic. The mould would need to be designed and then made in metal to very accurate tolerances. Precision engineering is of much greater importance today than the heavy engineering of many years ago.

Third angle views of a music cassette are given. With all the parts in their correct positions, draw to a scale of full size the following views:

a) a plan, the left hand half being a view with the top removed,

b) a front elevation, the left hand half being a section through centre line X-X (include the top),

c) an end elevation,

d) a view of the back.

Assume any dimensions not given; do not show hidden edges or dimensions.

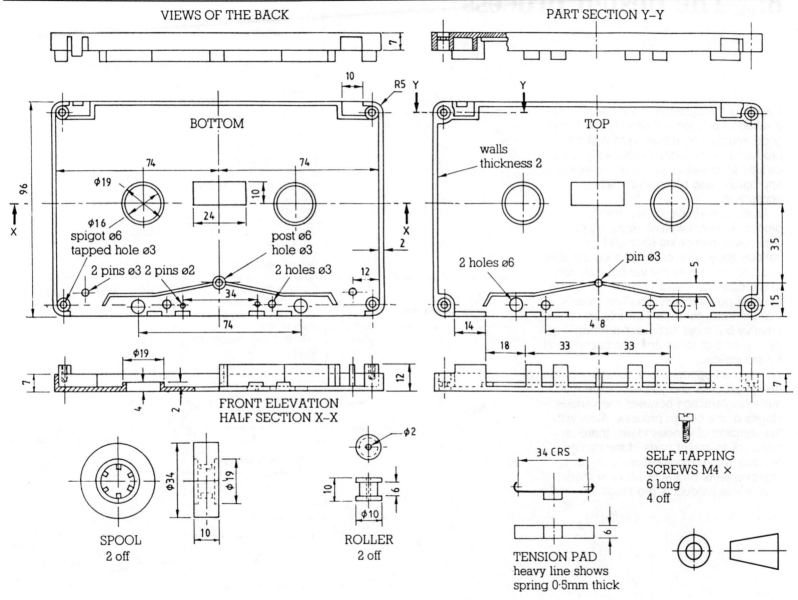

VIEWS OF THE BACK

PART SECTION Y–Y

BOTTOM

TOP

φ19
φ16
spigot ø6
tapped hole ø3

post ø6
hole ø3

2 pins ø3 2 pins ø2

2 holes ø3

walls
thickness 2

2 holes ø6

pin ø3

FRONT ELEVATION
HALF SECTION X–X

SPOOL
2 off

ROLLER
2 off

TENSION PAD
heavy line shows
spring 0·5mm thick

SELF TAPPING
SCREWS M4 ×
6 long
4 off

8. The design process

Design is the systematic approach to the solution of problems. Primarily the aim of good engineering design is to make a product that will function efficiently, cost as little as possible, be attractive where appropriate and be commercially acceptable.

Apart from simple cases, the design process is very involved requiring the services of numerous specialists in various fields. The designer must be able to select and reject the various solutions to a problem to enable him or her to find the best possible solution. This means that the designer must not only be creative but must also have a broad background of ideas and approaches and be self critical.

The chart opposite is a summary of the design process and you will notice that there is interaction between the various stages of the design process. Also, with the rejection of various ideas, there is feedback to earlier parts of the design process where modifications and improvements on the design are made, until a final product is produced.

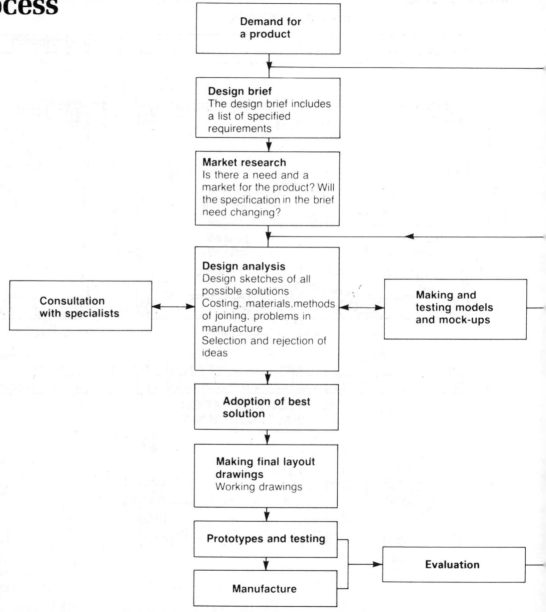

Demand for a product

An adjustable desk lamp will be used as an example of a simple product for illustrating the design process.

Is there a need for the product? Yes, a desk lamp would be used in offices, in the home and it could be useful for your own study. It could also be adapted for use with a drawing board. Many products that are designed today are based on existing products. For example different desk lamps do exist and at an early stage the designer would look at these products to try to work out the various advantages and disadvantages of each type. Clearly any new design for the desk lamp would need to be more attractive than those on the market at present, be reliable (serve the purpose for which it is designed) and be competitively priced.

Market research

At an early stage of the design process individuals and companies would be interviewed to find out what their requirements would be for a desk lamp. The results of the market research survey would then be analysed and important points would be incorporated in the design brief.

Design brief

The design brief is a statement of the design with a list specifying the requirements of the design. The following is an example.

Design a desk lamp.
Specification
1. It will fit on to a table.
2. The height and position of the lamp should be fully adjustable.
3. A shade will be used and the maximum lamp power will be 60 watt.
4. It should be attractive.
5. It should be reliable in operation and be electrically safe.
6. It should be easy to manufacture, using a variety of materials, and it should be competitively priced.

Design analysis

Keeping within the design brief, the designer now starts to investigate all the possible alternative solutions to this problem. Normally as many possible alternative solutions for each different part of the lamp would be produced. For example:

1. the base of the lamp,
2. methods of adjusting the height,
3. methods of adjusting the shade,
4. different ideas for the shade,
5. attaching the lamp fitting into the shade.

These are a few examples and in practice each one would be broken down even further.

At this stage there would be interaction between the designer and specialists concerning any problems with the design. For example the best materials to use, certain manufacturing processes and testing would be discussed. Many ideas will have been rejected before several possible alternative solutions are produced.

Models and mock-ups

Models and mock-ups of the various designs would be made to find out which design works best and also to give the designer an impression of what the product will look like.

A model is a scaled up or scaled down version of the object. It is made of any suitable material such as wood, expanded polystyrene, cardboard, etc. A model is cheap and quick to make, thus it helps prevent expensive mistakes at a later part of the design process.

A mock-up is a full size version of the design. For example a mock-up of the interior of a motor car may be made of wood, plaster and fibreglass to enable the designer to work out the best positions for seats, instruments, steering wheel, etc.

Production drawings

When the best solution has been adopted, detailed working drawings of all the individual parts of the lamp will be produced. This will also include assembly and sub-assembly drawings where necessary. All dimensions and thread sizes will be included together with a parts list indicating each individual part, its size and the material from which it is to be made. The drawings must give sufficient information for an engineer actually to make the lamp.

Prototype

Before manufacturing starts a single version of the lamp is actually made by an engineer according to the specifications on the production drawings. Whilst this may be a very costly exercise in terms of labour, considerable expense can be saved because any errors in the design will appear at this stage. If errors are found certain parts of the lamp will need to be redesigned.

Manufacture

Once all modifications have been made, various manufacturing companies would be asked to tender for manufacture of the table lamp. Initial production costs for setting up machinery can be high and to keep the cost of the lamp low many thousands would need to be mass produced. However the company that may be awarded the contract may not necessarily be the cheapest; other factors to be taken into account are reliability and quality control.

Evaluation

Does the product work? Does it satisfy all the requirements of the brief? Are people buying it or are there some unforeseen problems with it?

Design is a continuous process and good designers will always be looking for improvements on existing designs. A good designer, whilst having a wide educational background, should be self critical and forward looking in his or her approach.

9. Materials

It is essential for design work that the designer has a working knowledge of the common materials used in manufacturing, engineering and construction.

Different materials have different properties such as strength, conductivity of heat and electricity, cost, ease of joining, whether they are flexible or rigid, metals and non-metals. The tables in this chapter are a summary of the various properties of different materials and their uses.

Metals

Metals are produced from ores which are extracted from the earth. They are processed by chemical and electrolytic means to produce the pure metal which is an element, for example copper. Some of these metals are combined chemically to produce alloys such as brass which is made from copper and zinc. Metals are classified into two main groups: ferrous metals which contain iron and non ferrous metals which do not contain iron.

Sizes of metals

The table on the right shows the common cross-sectional shapes and sizes of metals.

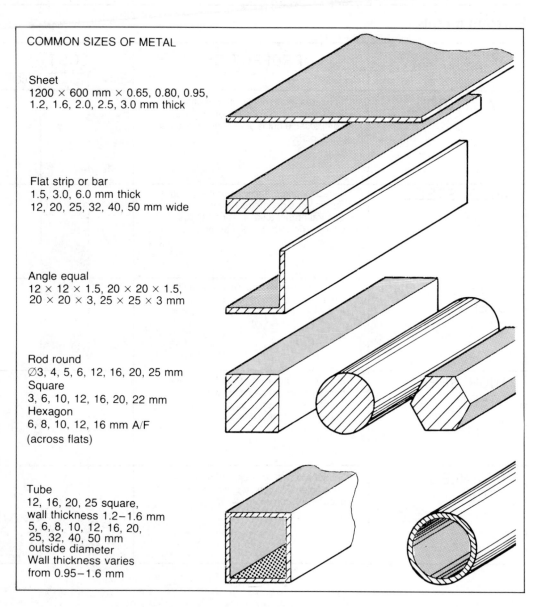

COMMON SIZES OF METAL

Sheet
1200 × 600 mm × 0.65, 0.80, 0.95, 1.2, 1.6, 2.0, 2.5, 3.0 mm thick

Flat strip or bar
1.5, 3.0, 6.0 mm thick
12, 20, 25, 32, 40, 50 mm wide

Angle equal
12 × 12 × 1.5, 20 × 20 × 1.5, 20 × 20 × 3, 25 × 25 × 3 mm

Rod round
∅3, 4, 5, 6, 12, 16, 20, 25 mm
Square
3, 6, 10, 12, 16, 20, 22 mm
Hexagon
6, 8, 10, 12, 16 mm A/F
(across flats)

Tube
12, 16, 20, 25 square,
wall thickness 1.2–1.6 mm
5, 6, 8, 10, 12, 16, 20,
25, 32, 40, 50 mm
outside diameter
Wall thickness varies
from 0.95–1.6 mm

Ferrous metals

METAL	PROPERTIES	COST			USES
		LOW		HIGH	
CAST IRON	Is poured into moulds when molten to form castings. Strong under compression but is very brittle. Contains 3.5% carbon	▓			General heavy engineering: machine parts, brackets, engine blocks, motors, gratings, stoves, boilers, pipe couplings
MILD STEEL	Can be worked easily, is malleable and ductile. Has good strength and is a general purpose steel. Tends to rust easily. Iron with 0.25% carbon		▓		General fabrication: frameworks, domestic products, brackets
HIGH CARBON STEEL	Not so malleable and ductile as mild steel; it can be hardened and tempered. Iron which contains 0.7 – 1.5% carbon		▓		Hand tools, saws, chisels, screwdrivers, farming tools, springs
HIGH SPEED STEEL	Self hardening even at red heat. Very hard and cannot be easily worked. Carbon steel which has been alloyed with 18% tungsten			▓	Drills, lathe tools, milling cutters
STAINLESS STEEL	Fairly hard, will not rust and retains a good finish Carbon steel which contains about 12% chromium			▓	Cutlery, dishes, sinks, furniture and frameworks

Non-ferrous metals

METAL	PROPERTIES	COST		USES
		LOW	HIGH	
BRASS	Quite strong and ductile, works easily and can be soldered. An alloy, copper with 35% zinc	▓		Plumbing fittings, screws, decorative ironmongery on furniture, gear wheels in precision instruments, electrical fittings
BRONZE	Is often in the form of castings. It is strong and tough and resists corrosion. Copper with 10% tin	▓		Bearings, gears, propellors for ships
COPPER	Works well, is a good conductor of heat and electricity. Can be soldered and brazed and accepts a high polish	▓		Water pipes and electrical cables
ALUMINIUM	Works well, very soft and ductile, resists corrosion, is very light in weight. It is often alloyed to increase strength	▓		Kitchen and engine parts. Alloys such as duralium are much stronger and are used for aircraft parts, also general castings
NICKEL	Hard metal which is resistant to corrosion		▓	Plating of steel screws to provide an attractive finish and a protection against rust
SILVER	Resistant to corrosion, soft and forms well. Good surface finish and conductor of electricity		▓	Jewellery and electrical contacts
GOLD	As silver but more expensive		▓	Jewellery and electrical contacts
ZINC	Soft metal that forms a protective oxide coating	▓		Galvanising iron and steel to prevent rusting. Also used in torch cells and the manufacture of brass
TIN	Expensive metal with a bright shiny finish. Resistant to corrosion	▓		Main use is for plating steel (tinplate) for food cans
LEAD	Low melting point, very soft and dense	▓		Motor car batteries and is the main constituent of solder. Used for flashing on roofs. No longer used for water pipes

Non-metals

MATERIAL	PROPERTIES	COST			USES
		LOW		HIGH	
TIMBER	Most timbers can be worked easily, they are strong and reasonably priced. They will accept a good quality finish and can be very attractive. There are two main types of timber: softwoods which come from cone bearing trees and hardwoods which come from deciduous trees	▓			General constructional work and furniture
PLASTICS	Plastics are of great importance in the world of modern technology. Most plastics are derived from oil, thus their high cost. They can be easily formed and moulded. Some are very strong when reinforced (fibreglass). Some are transparent (perspex). Polyethylene is a plastic which is very resilient (withstands shock)		▓		Bakelite for electrical fittings, fibreglass for boat hulls and insulation, polystyrene can be vacuum formed to make trays for packaging, expanded polystyrene is used for insulation and packaging, PVC for pipes and general mouldings, polyethylene for buckets and bowls
CERAMICS	Ceramics are products that are manufactured from silica or sand. They tend to be very dense and brittle. They are poor conductors of heat and electricity. Some ceramics are opaque (pot) whilst others can be transparent (glass)			▓	Glass products, electrical insulators, cement products, concrete, bricks, pots, sanitary ware, crockery, tiles and spark plugs
RUBBER	Rubber is a natural material which is manufactured from the latex of the rubber tree. In its natural form it is very sticky and unstable. Plasticisers are added to make the rubber harder. Rubber will stretch (elastic) and will compress. Rubber is attacked by chemicals and will harden with excess heat		▓		Conveyor and vee belts, flexible couplings, shock absorbers, tyres, engine mountings. Footware, hoses and tubes. It was once used for electrical insulation on cables but plastic is now more common because it is cheaper and does not perish with age

Index